CLASSIC SHIPS

CLASSIC SHIPS

• ROMANCE AND REALITY •

NICHOLAS FAITH

B⬦XTREE

In Association with Channel Four Television Corporation

First published in Great Britain in 1995 by Boxtree Limited

Text © Nicholas Faith 1995

The right of Nicholas Faith to be identified as Author of this Work has been asserted by him in accordance
with the Copyright, Designs and Patents Act 1988.

1 3 5 7 9 10 8 6 4 2

Designed by Robert Updegraff
Printed and bound in Italy by Graphicom, Vicenza for

Boxtree Limited
Broadwall House
21 Broadwall
London   SE1 9PL

A CIP catalogue entry for this book is available from the British Library.

ISBN 0 7522 1022 X

Classic Ships accompanies the Channel Four series 'Classic Ships' produced by Uden Associates.

Half title page: Brunel's *Great Britain* on her maiden voyage. In the six years it took to build, the designer greatly
modified the ship, transforming it from a wooden paddle-steamer to one with a screw propeller and iron keel.
Title page: Tug boats are still essential workboats. This one is seen at the German port of Bremerhaven in 1987.

CONTENTS

ACKNOWLEDGEMENTS

This book would not have been possible without the backing of Peter Grimsdale and Susanna Yager at Channel Four. The team responsible for the television series of the same name – Patrick Uden, Michael Proudfoot, Jo O'Mahony, Philip Martin, Senara Wilson, Chris Durlacher and Jess Whitehead – were more helpful than perhaps they realized. Ian and Richard Johnstone-Bryden kindly read through several of the chapters. At Boxtree, Susanna Wadeson, Katy Carrington, Anna Kingsley, Caroline North and the designer, Robert Updegraff, coped magnificently with a dauntingly tight publishing schedule, and with an author who was, it has to be admitted, sometimes tense and grumpy. Thank you all.

The 440-ton *Craigantlet* after running aground in 1982 during a storm near the lighthouse at Stranraer on the extreme south-west tip of Scotland. It didn't help matters that her cargo included dangerous chemicals.

INTRODUCTION

In the beginning, man sat astride a log and floated on lakes and rivers. The next step in the conquest of water was to bind two logs together and sit on them. This demanded less sophistication than that possessed even by the most primitive Bronze Age peoples. As civilizations developed, many shapes and sizes of ship, from hollowed-out tree trunks serving as canoes to coracles made of skins stretched over a wooden frame and square-rigged ships of every shape and size, are to be found throughout recorded history in otherwise very different cultures across the world. Of course, from the beginning there were variations, but these were largely the result of the need to rely on available materials, which is why, for example, the early Egyptians used reeds for their floats, while the Assyrians' *kelleks* featured layers of timber supported by inflated animal skins.

The next step, the specialist ship, was a matter of necessity combined with technical possibilities, and its existence and increasing complexity was a symbol of progress. Bronze Age man, unlike his predecessors in the Stone Age, had axes and saws with which to shape wood into planks and no longer had to rely on hollowing out tree trunks. The need for specialization was itself a result of increasing sophistication as the trading patterns sprang from surplusses of agricultural products, thanks to irrigation in such favoured regions as the Valley of the Nile. 'Alongside the weavers, potters and smiths,' wrote Charles

Gibson, 'the Bronze Age produced another specialist – the professional sailor.'[1] For man has always been the essential element in the world of ships. The ship can be a thing of beauty, from the yacht to the mammoth liner which, in the words of the poet John Masefield, 'marches across great oceans like a queen'. But, as Gibson so rightly insists, 'without men there would be no ships . . . the ship has no existence outside human society'.

Over the millennia the ship has remained a symbol, a mark of the progress of civilization. More recently, and, more narrowly, it has marked the status of a country's industry and society; indeed, the history of ships and shipping echoes that of the civilizations which gave rise to it. In the thirteenth century the Chinese junk was a finer, more advanced vessel than anything found in Western Europe at the time. But Chinese society, in shipping as in so many other instances, was too hidebound to exploit its lead, even though its early ships contained many of the elements which culminated in that nineteenth-century masterpiece, the clipper.

The story of British ships and shipping in more recent centuries bears some superficial resemblance to that of the Chinese. An era of industrial supremacy was followed by a longer period of ineluctable decline into a post-industrial society. It is not surprising that the British, none of whom lived further than 80 miles (129km) from the sea, should

The late Victorian leisure revolution: during the first wave of female emancipation even respectable ladies could indulge in strenuous exercise.

The D-day commemoration at Portsmouth brought together many of the world's ships great and small, including the QEII which can just be seen behind the mighty American aircraft-carrier, *George Washington*.

Opposite: Once upon a time, Saville Road in London's Docklands had a dry dock at the end of it. Now it backs on to the terminal buildings of London's City Airport.

Ships of the home fleet on patrol in 1940: virtually all of them were veterans of the First World War.

have evolved with a peculiar consciousness of its presence and an awareness of being an island race. This national trait was also a matter of brutal necessity: like other island people, such as the Japanese, and like the Dutch, imprisoned behind their dykes, the British needed to command the seas to survive, to obtain the food and raw materials they could not provide for themselves.

Before embarking on any lament for a vanished golden age one must remember that British supremacy was relatively short-lived. Back in the seventeenth century the Dutch dominated the seas, building far more types of specialized vessel than the British, including such long-lasting designs as the schooner. The rise of the British merchant navy only really began during the reign of Charles II. When he came to the throne in 1660, British trade amounted to an average of 93,000 tons*, two-thirds of it carried in British vessels. By the end of the Napoleonic Wars it had risen to 2.7 million tons, over four-fifths British-borne.

Even then Britain was by no means dominant. In the first decades of the nineteenth century the Americans built the first steamboats, and continued to build schooners and clippers far finer than anyone else's. But they lost the lead after the Civil War, when they turned inward to their own fast-expanding economy. As a result they did not have the same need for shipping as Britain, with its relentless and ever-increasing import trade.

If Britain's late-Victorian dominance was a reflection of the country's general standing at the time, so the decline of British shipping, and above all of British shipbuilding, was symptomatic of our general deindustrialization. Yet we can now perceive a new wave – the return of the shipbuilder,

not as an industrialist but as a craftsman, running with a social and economic tide combining greater leisure, a desire to pit human forces against Nature and the realization that small can be profitable as well as beautiful. For although British shipping and shipbuilding are a veritable bomb site, among the ruins there are new hopefuls as well as survivors of older traditions. These, to me, are the most romantic elements in the story. For as C.R. Benstead says, 'Evolution is a commonplace, a yielding to changing circumstance in order to survive, and there is nothing meritorious about that. What is outstanding is

The boat which is crashing through the 'Roaring Forties' – south of the fortieth latitude – in the 1993–94 Whitbread Round the World Race is called by the curious name of *Intrum Justitia*, after its sponsor, a European debt-collecting agency.

Opposite: The face of modern ocean racing: the *Hetman* at Punta del Este in December 1993 in the Whitbread Round the World Race.

Overleaf: A memory of past bustle: Thames sailing barges after the Second World War.

survival without evolution.'[2] In the case of Britain, he cites the Humber keel, which hardly changed in a thousand years; indeed, it was 'not very different from the ceolas that brought Hengist and Horsa to Kent in AD 449'.

This book, and the related television series, reflect the new reality. They are a hymn to living vessels, to the people who cherish new boats, and those which have been lovingly restored, and who sail them: sailmakers, boatbuilders, dockers and the crews. They also provide social history, giving some sense of the lives of those who sail in ships.

To try to give a focus within such an enormous subject I have, in general, confined myself to the past 150 years, starting in the 1840s, when steam power first made a major impact. But the book is not confined to the television series it is designed to accompany; it is complementary, and covers a much broader canvas. Nevertheless, I have deliberately omitted many types of boat, including (and especially) the appallingly designed and highly dangerous roll-on, roll-off ferries which are most people's only contact with vessels larger than a dinghy.

Of course – and this is one of the fascinations of the subject – there is a considerable overlap between types of ships. Boats originally used commercially have been transformed to suit leisure purposes and in both world wars merchant ships were as involved as their escorts. Some of the boats in Chapter 6 are the smaller, cheaper and less ambitious siblings of the classic yachts described in Chapter 7. There is a much clearer link between seamen themselves than between their ships, and one which connects everyone who ventures out on to water, be it ocean, sea, estuary or river, however tame that water may appear to be to the casual observer. Not surprisingly, after writing this book I ended up with an even greater admiration for the men and women who 'go down to the sea in ships' than I had when I began to work on it.

* The conversion of tons into the metric equivalent of tonnes has been omitted throughout to avoid confusion, since the imperial and metric measurements are so similar.

Mike Cooper

CLASSIC SHIPS

MEN O' WAR

·I·

BRITAIN'S ROYAL NAVY embodies the national consciousness of invulnerability which arises from the country's status as an island. The ships surrounding that island in turn encapsulate a whole host of traditions – hearts of oak, ready, aye, ready and the like. The tradition of a specialized navy, as opposed to one composed of merchant ships adapted for warlike purposes, goes back to the reign of Henry VII at the end of the fifteenth century. At the time Britain was a minor power, at sea as on land, and naval battles were essentially infantry battles fought at sea, since contemporary cannon lacked the range for effective use at any distance. But by the time of the Spanish Armada at the end of the sixteenth century, naval vessels had become increasingly specialized and converted merchant ships were of little use.

Naval vessels were soon categorized, running from 'first rates' with more than eighty cannon (by the eighteenth century they often carried over a hundred) down to the humble 'sixth rates' which had fewer than twelve. They were supported by frigates, designed for speed and hitting power, not to take punishment in that all their armament was carried on the upper deck, and not, as with larger ships, below deck. By Napoleonic times these ships were largely standardized and were fully rigged. Such ships, in capable hands, could cope with any weather conditions. For the first time coasts could be watched the whole year round, as Lord St Vincent showed when his fleet blockaded the French port of Brest. The result was that the French fleet was

largely immobilized. As he put it, 'I do not say the French cannot come, I only say they cannot come by sea.'

The tradition of seamanship and craftsmanship is summed up in Nelson's flagship HMS *Victory*. As John Keegan put it:

> The visitor will immediately understand the phrase, 'a wooden world' . . . Wood surrounds and encloses him: planed and scrubbed boards of pine or teak eight inches wide under his feet, sawn baulks of oak a foot and a half square running athwartships overhead, hanging 'knees' cut from whole tree forks at his elbow and pillars of fir, too large for a man's arm to encircle, breaking the deck's run where masts descend to meet the wooden keel (and rise to bear the hamper of wooden yards, tops and crosstrees high over poop, waist and forecastle in the open air above.)'[1]

The result was colossally strong, able to cope with any existing solid shot even from 32-pounders (14.5kg). They could bring masts crashing to the deck, kill the crew, let in the sea, but otherwise the wood would simply absorb the shock – in Keegan's words, 'It was "man-killing" not "ship-killing" that won the Battle of Trafalgar.' The ship was a self-contained world with its own carpenters, butchers, painters, sailmakers and hairdressers. More crucially, and notably unlike its steam-powered successors, it did not require refuelling and could therefore stay on station at sea for months on end. As Keegan says: 'The successors of the wooden man

A frigate under construction at Swan Hunter's historic shipyard on Tyneside before it was closed in an orgy of government industrial destructiveness, even though finanicial aid was available from the European Union.

of war would go further, shoot further and hit harder than anything wrought from oak . . . but no product of the ship-wright's art . . . would ever serve the purposes of those who pay and those who command so narrowly.' Napoleon could never come to terms, psychologically as well as militarily, with the superiority of Nelson's navy. His only recorded comment on the Battle of Trafalgar was that 'Storms caused us the loss of several ships after an imprudently undertaken engagement.'

Nevertheless, within half a century of Trafalgar the old world had been swept away by the arrival of steam. In 1843 the Admiralty conducted a famous trial between a paddle-steamer and the sailing sloop *Rattler* which had been converted into a steam-powered vessel using a propeller rather than paddle wheels. After a gigantic tug of war the *Rattler* won. Ten years later the Crimean War, coming after the Russians had used shells to destroy a Turkish fleet at Sinope in 1851, completed their lordships' conversion to the virtues

The Battle of Trafalgar: Nelson's revolutionary tactics involved breaking through the line of the combined French and Spanish fleets.

Warrior, the warship that changed the world. It was built of iron, had a screw propeller, was heavily armoured, and its guns fired shells rather than round shot. All revolutionary stuff for 1851.

of steam power – as well as to those of armour plate and of hollow shells filled with high explosive.

The first sign of the conversion was a revolutionary warship, the ironclad *Warrior*, which was built in 1860 on the Thames. It was inspired by the French ship *La Gloire*. The *Warrior*, wrote Keegan, was 'steam-propelled, shell-firing, iron in construction from keel to bulwarks and heavily armoured as well. Seeing her lying at anchor beside the surviving wooden walls of the Channel Fleet, Palmerston [the British prime minister] said that she looked "like a black snake among the rabbits".' Speeds increased: by 1873, *Devastation*, the first warship built without sails, achieved 14 knots, and by 1879 two cruisers, *Iris* and *Mercury*, had been built entirely of iron. ('Cruiser', originally 'cruising ship', replaced the old name 'frigate'.)

The next leap forward in naval history came forty years later in the naval race that dominated the fifteen years before the outbreak of the First World War. It was set off by Kaiser Wilhelm II of Germany, who was sufficiently obsessed by the ocean to spend years at sea himself. It took a fiery revolutionary, First Sea Lord 'Jackie' Fisher, to dynamite British naval traditions – once memorably described as 'rum, sodomy and the lash' by the then First Lord of the Admiralty Winston Churchill, Fisher's friend and supporter. Paul Kennedy wrote:

For Fisher, efficiency, firepower, speed, economy and a concentration of force were the key yardsticks with which to measure the fighting capacity of a navy. From this point of view nothing was more preposterous than the maintenance of vast numbers of slow, obsolescent cruisers and gunboats all over the globe, wasting money and especially men. In time of war, he argued, 'An enemy cruiser would lap them up like an armadillo let loose on an ant-hill.'[2]

With a handful of exceptions, the gunboats beloved of arm-chair imperialists were, in Fisher's own words, 'merely the symbol of the power of a nation, not a concrete embodi-ment of it'. As a result he ruthlessly scrapped hundreds of obsolescent ships. Although his revolution covered every aspect of naval life – according to Kennedy, 'dockyards, pay, officer entry and training, service conditions, gunnery and general efficiency were all improved under Fisher's drive' – the heart of the matter lay in the previous concentration of men and money in what Fisher saw as hundreds of useless packets of small, slow and usually superannuated vessels scattered throughout the seven seas. With the money he saved by dispensing with these ships, he 'inaugurated a new round of battleship construction which consigned all existing types to obsolescence', as Keegan puts it.

Fisher also inaugurated a policy of not expecting his capital ships – battleships and other large warships – to fight every type of opponent. Instead they were to rely on their big guns and leave escorts to combat smaller enemy vessels. More importantly, the new ships – German, French and American as well as British – had turbine engines where the blades revolved, rather than reciprocating engines in which power came from the up-and-down movement of the engine's pistons. The turbine, as developed by Charles Parsons, had blades like nozzles arranged on a shaft in parallel rows. Its main advantage over the reciprocating steam engine lay in its simplicity: it was lighter, occupied less space and used less steam, qualities which reduced the depth of the engine room and thus greatly diminished the need for armour.

Parsons patented his first turbine in 1884, though this lacked a condenser which increased the turbine's efficiency by using the energy released when steam converts back into water. With one it could drive a dynamo at 18,000rpm. In 1894 he fitted his new-fangled engine into the 44.5-ton *Turbinia*. On trials she sailed at under 20 knots, but it was soon perceived that the propeller was revving too fast and expending too much of its energy on tearing holes in the water as opposed to actually powering the ship. Two years later the vessel was re-engined with three turbines revolving more slowly, each driving a single propeller. It reached 34.5 knots, easily a record, and made such good use of the steam that after leaving the boiler at 250lb per sq in pressure was down to 150psi before entering the cylinder and the exhaust was a mere 1psi.

Yet Parsons' turbine was not taken seriously until he exposed the backwardness of contemporary naval thinking in the most public and humiliating fashion possible by liter-ally running rings round the navy's finest, assembled at the great Naval Review held at Spithead in 1897 to mark Queen Victoria's Diamond Jubilee. As a result, turbines were fitted to two destroyers within a couple of years. In 1904 special comparative trials were made between two light cruisers, one fitted with reciprocating engines, the other with turbines. The turbine-engined *Amethyst* reached full speed with a coal consumption 30 per cent less than the *Topaz* with its orthodox engines, and, what is more, provided 40 per cent more power. Three years later the Admiralty adopted the turbine for every type of warship.

A parallel decision to switch fuel from coal to oil was greatly delayed by a typical muddle over trials carried out in 1902, in which their lordships ignored expert advice and used obsolete burners. Nevertheless, well before 1914 the fleet was being converted to oil burning, a process which led to Winston Churchill's decision as First Lord of the Admiralty to control Britain's sources of oil by investing in the Anglo–Persian Oil Company, the predecessor of British Petroleum.

Progress was so fast that everyone involved, from Fisher to the Kaiser, shared a delusion that they could have every-thing, that a 'fast capital ship' could combine the strength and firepower of a battleship with the speed of a cruiser. In fact warship design continued to entail a series of trade-offs to balance speed, size and the weight of armour. Designers

Turbinia at speed. It was Sir Charles Parson's turbine engine, not the ship's rather unremarkable shape, that made it revolutionary.

had also learned the wrong lessons from the success of the Japanese in their conflict with the Russians, particularly at the Battle of Tsushima in 1905. It did indeed prove that new guns were effective at hitherto undreamed of ranges, but, as Anthony Preston says: 'The most important lesson of all went unheeded. Examination of both Japanese and Russian ships showed that damage below the waterline caused progressive flooding, and as many compartments were only theoretically watertight, it was possible for a ship to sink much faster than expected.'[3]

The lesson was ignored but with a speed which seems inconceivable today, the *Dreadnought*, the model for dozens of ships constructed in the following decade, was produced. It took only a year to build and commission from the date its keel was laid at Portsmouth, 2 October 1905. In January 1907 it left for a shakedown cruise. No problems were apparent: it was, wrote Preston, 'more robustly and rationally armoured than any ship afloat, armed exclusively with armour-cracking guns'. As a result of Fisher's policy of concentrating the fire-power of major new ships, *Dreadnought* was provided with ten

HMS *Dreadnought,* the truly awesome precursor of a noble line.

Iron Duke in action against the Bolsheviks at Kaffa Bay in the Black Sea. Part of the British effort to support the anti-Soviet 'White' forces.

12in (30.5cm) guns in five turrets, twenty-four 12-pounders (5.5kg) for use against torpedo boats and four submerged torpedo tubes. Other advances included fuses which would delay ignition until the shell had passed through the target's armour, as well as great improvements in range-finding optics. In addition, Fisher's ally Admiral Percy Scott increased the percentage of hits from 30 to 80 largely by introducing centralized gun control.

Dreadnought's greatest moment came in March 1915, when it rammed and sank the U-boat which had been responsible for scuttling three cruisers. But progress in battleship design – especially developments in speed, which made *Dreadnought*'s successors superior in this area – had been so quick that by July 1916, in Randolph Pears' words, 'she left the Grand Fleet for good. She had become too slow to maintain the speed of the fleet.'[4] The Germans immediately took up the challenge and once the British realized that they planned to build sixteen capital ships

between 1908 and 1911, thus leaving Britain with an advantage of only four, there was a 'naval scare'. The cry, 'We want eight and we won't wait' gave rise to another of Churchill's famous aphorisms: 'The Admiralty had demanded six ships; the economists offered four; and we finally compromised on eight.'

The first departure from the design of *Dreadnought* was HMS *Neptune*, completed in January 1911. The deck was armoured against attack by aircraft and it was the first ship to have gun turrets superimposed on each other. Four 22,500-ton ships of the Orion class, all completed in 1912, marked a much more important step forward, for they were the first to carry the new 13.5in (34.3cm) guns and the first to have all their guns mounted on the centre line. The next year four more improved Orion-class ships, the King George V class, were built and another four appeared in 1914. One of them, the *Iron Duke*, became famous as Sir John Jellicoe's flagship during the 1916 Battle of Jutland

The Royal Navy at
Spithead, off the Isle of
Wight just before the
outbreak of war in 1914:
the largest and most
powerful fleet of
battleships ever
assembled in one spot.

Destroyers rushing back to Portsmouth harbour in 1914 past HMS *Victory*.

(the only time at which the whole Grand Fleet was deployed against Germany). At 30,000 tons fully loaded they were bigger, and as well as the usual ten 13.5in big guns they also carried twelve 6in (15.25cm) guns as protection against the longer-range torpedos then being developed.

Within a year of the outbreak of war the navy was commissioning the first of five battleships of the Queen Elizabeth class, which marked a quantum leap forward from the *Dreadnought* and its successors. These were the first battleships to burn oil rather than coal; they were bigger still (33,000 tons fully loaded) and more heavily armoured; they were also faster – at 25 knots they could keep up with the fastest battlecruisers. The new giants also mounted eight of the new 15in (38cm) guns, which had been successfully put into production even before a test gun had been built. These guns were monsters: 57ft (17.4m) long and weighing 97 tons, and capable of hurling a 1-ton shell up to 20 miles (32km).

Progress bred progress. With a 15in gun it was possible to drop one twin gun turret and the ship could still launch a

broadside of 15,000lb (6,804kg): nearly 8 tons of shells, more firepower than ten of the latest 13.5in guns. The space left vacant could be filled with more boilers. The design of this new class was so advanced that the ships survived until the Second World War. Only one, *Barham*, was sunk and *Warspite* fought in both the Pacific and the Mediterranean, where she served as the flagship of Lord Cunningham of Hyndhope. As he put it in a metaphor which could serve as an epitaph for the whole class: 'When the old lady lifts her skirts she can still run.'

The speed and strength of the Queen Elizabeth class spelled the end of that peculiar hybrid the battlecruiser, which sacrificed protection to speed in its role of sweeping away the shield of the enemy's battle fleet. The first battlecruisers were three Invincible-class ships completed in 1908, which were unable to withstand concentrated fire from heavy guns at close range. By the time war broke out progress had been so pell-mell that categories had become thoroughly confused. 'When the Lion class were built in 1909–12,' writes

Preston, 'they were some 4,000 tons bigger and over 100ft [30.5m] longer than their battleship equivalent, the Orion class. These anomalies led to the introduction of the term "battleship cruiser" and finally "battlecruiser", while the popular press [indiscriminately] termed them and the Orions "superdreadnoughts".'

Effectively there were seven of the final version of these 'superdreadnoughts' all more heavily armed (and armoured) than their predecessors: *Lion, Princess Royal* and *Queen Mary* all weighed 26,350 tons and mounted eight 13.5in guns (where the Invincibles had only 12-inchers); *Hood*, completed only after the end of the war and chiefly memorable for its discomfort and the inadequate horizontal protection which led to its being sunk by Bismarck in 1941 with the loss of all but three of her crew; *Renown* and *Repulse*. Finally, there was the 28,500-ton *Tiger*, to John Keegan 'the most beautiful ship ever built and the last battlecruiser to be built before the whole breed was superseded by the faster battleships of the Queen Elizabeth class'. *Tiger* was superbly designed: its eight 13.5in guns were better arranged than in *Lion*; it had four submerged 12in torpedo tubes, 9in (22.9cm) armour and better-designed boilers giving a speed of 35 knots.

December 8th 1941 marked the end of the battleship era. The black blobs are sailors hoping to be rescued by a destroyer after torpedos from Japanese aircraft had sunk the *Prince of Wales* and the *Repulse*. Despite the rescue efforts, 2,320 seamen drowned.

HMS *Tiger*. Whether you call it a battlecruiser or a superdreadnought, it's hard to disagree with John Keegan's verdict that this was the most beautiful warship ever built.

Murmansk convoy under attack: a scene which was only too typical for the ships taking supplies to Russia between 1941 and 1945.

All these ships, and many more, fought in the Battle of Jutland, the greatest ever fought between such numbers of battleships. Yet this indecisive encounter showed the limits of their power and provided a hint of the very different shape of things to come. It was a German, Vice-Admiral Hoffman, who foresaw the future in a private letter he wrote a few days after the battle. 'The result, incidentally, strengthens my conviction that the days of superdread-noughts are numbered. It is senseless to build 30,000-ton ships which cannot defend themselves against a torpedo shot.' The torpedos were often fired from U-boats, and as a result, in Kennedy's words, 'the whole operation turned Jellicoe's great unease about the menace posed by the U-boats to his battleships into a virtual obsession'.

The weight restrictions imposed on all the world's navies by the Treaty of Washington in 1921 provided designers with a ten-year breathing space in which they learned to reduce weight and improve machinery and gun control in time for the next arms race in the late 1930s. In the circumstances it was easier to change armaments (two Italian ships converted from 35- to 100-ton guns overnight), but it took years to

redesign ships to carry the heavier armour which accounted for up to a third of a battleship's weight. The speed-weight-armour-armament equation was further complicated by the restrictions laid down in Washington, the most obvious upshot being the artificial limitation of *Nelson* and *Rodney*, the two major ships built by Britain in the early 1930s, to 33,900 tons. As they had to be cut down from 48,000 tons they looked rather unbalanced thereafter, with all their nine 16in (40.6cm) guns mounted forward. They were heavily armoured to lessen their vulnerability to bombs, albeit at the expense of speed. In the older *Renown* and *Repulse*, on the other hand, armour was sacrificed for speed, and these 15in-gun ships were capable of 29 knots compared with 23 for the *Nelson*. Meanwhile, although the German pocket battleships had both speed and armour packed into a nominal 10,000 tons displacement, they carried only 12in guns.

After the restrictions imposed by the naval treaties of the 1920s and early 1930s had been removed, building began anew. The British admitted learning from the Germans, implicitly anyway, in the construction of the five ships of the King George V class laid down in 1937. They carried ten

14in (35.6cm) guns and sixteen 5.25in (13.3cm) quick-firing guns, but their theoretically superior armour proved inadequate when one of them, *Prince of Wales*, was destroyed by Japanese torpedos in the Second World War. The limit was reached in the early 1940s with a handful of monsters of between 40 and 45,000 tons – *Vanguard*, the last British battleship, weighed in at 42,500 tons.

The era when big was beautiful lasted until 1941. Then came three dramatic events. The first was the sinking in May of that year of one of the finest battleships ever built, the *Bismarck*, which weighed at least 40,000 tons, provided remarkable armour protection and produced a speed of no less than 35 knots. After an epic battle involving four British battleships (one of which, *Hood*, was sunk), *Bismarck* was crippled by the last of seventy-one torpedos fired from a handful of antiquated Swordfish aircraft. As Sydney Poole put it:

It had taken forty-eight ships of all sizes to hunt down this one raider, including six battleships, three battle-cruisers, more than half the capital ship strength with which the navy had entered the war, as well as the two Fleet aircraft carriers, but, even so, the *Bismarck* would have reached safety but for the damage given to her by *Prince of Wales* and *Ark Royal*'s aircraft.[5]

The supremacy of air power was rubbed in by the Japanese success over the American battleships moored at Pearl Harbor, and finally confirmed the next day by the sinking of two of Britain's proudest battleships, the *Prince of Wales* and the *Repulse*, by Japanese dive-bombers. It was entirely appropriate that Tom Phillips, the British admiral who exposed his ships with such tragic foolhardiness, had previously scorned the importance of air power at sea. But the Admiralty had learned the lesson. Building battleships took

HMS *Nelson* owed its lop-sided appearance to treaty restrictions which reduced its weight from a planned 45,000 tons to 33,500 tons. Nevertheless, its 16in guns were mightily impressive. It needed an acre of cane to provide the sugar for the cordite used in a single round.

very low priority from then on, for the mighty *Vanguard*, laid down in October 1941, was not completed until 1946.

The coda to the battleship era was provided when the biggest of them all, Japan's 72,000-ton *Yamato*, was sunk by bombs and torpedos from American carrier-borne aircraft. Like the mighty German *Tirpitz*, she never fired her massive main armament against enemy battleships. 'When she went down,' wrote the American naval historian Samuel Eliot Morison, 'five centuries of naval warfare ended.'[6] After 1945 only the Americans could permit themselves the luxury of maintaining ships like the 45,000-ton Iowa, whose 16in (40.6cm) guns were used in 1983 to bombard shore positions in Beirut. The only effect was to embitter the conflict.

Neither of the major naval battlegrounds of the Second World War involved battleships as primary weapon systems. The most important, the naval war in the Pacific, was fought out largely between aircraft-carriers. In the later stages of the war American battleships acted almost entirely as mobile gun platforms to help amphibious landings – a valuable role, but not a primary one, nor the one for which they had been so expensively built. As Paul Kennedy wrote: 'It is, in fact, difficult to discover many naval engagements of the Second World War whose results were not decidedly influenced by the use of aircraft.'

The principal role of the Royal Navy in the Second World War was far less glamorous. It was to protect convoys in the Atlantic, the North Sea and on the run to northern Russia through the Norwegian Sea. This involved fighting two types of ship: the seemingly ubiquitous U-boats and the speedy German raiders which escaped from port to harass shipping the world over. These dangers could range from cruisers, like the Emden, which had terrorized the whole eastern part of the Indian Ocean early in the First World War, to 'pocket battleships' supposedly of only 10,000 tons, and the *Scharnhorst* and *Gneisenau*, two 32,000-ton battle-cruisers with nine 11in guns which posed such a threat in the Second World War. Even now the long, grim struggle for control of the Atlantic has never received the recognition it deserved. For those involved, the war between the

slow, inadequately defended convoys of merchant men and the German U-boats, which often operated in 'wolf packs' in the mid-Atlantic or off the Norwegian coast, was the maritime equivalent of the war in the trenches on the Western Front in the Great War.

The Battle of the Atlantic was based on one simple fact: Britain not only imported all its oil, half its food and almost all its high-grade metal ores, but it also did so from a long way away. The prewar policy of Empire Free Trade made excellent political sense, but in wartime it merely multiplied Britain's vulnerability. Typically, British imports were carried over twice as far as their French equivalents.

The battle was fought between the 300 U-boats finally assembled by Admiral Doenitz and ten times as many British merchant men, a fleet which was still the biggest in the world, but only three-quarters of the size (in carrying capacity as well as numbers) it had been a quarter of a century earlier at the outbreak of the First World War. In the course of the battle, over 2,600 merchant ships were sunk with the loss of 30,000 lives, but by the end of the war seven out of ten of Doenitz's U-boat crews, 28,000 out of a hand-picked force numbering 40,000, had been killed, a far higher death rate than in any other sector of war.

The bitter, unforgiving tone of the conflict was set immediately war broke out. The Royal Navy had laid all its plans on the assumption that the Germans would carry on unrestricted submarine warfare, as they had done in the First World War. They were proved right in the first days of hostilities when a U-boat torpedoed and sank the liner *Athenia*, which was carrying civilian passengers. The U-boat captain claimed that he thought that the liner was carrying troops.

Again, as in the trenches of the First World War, the nature of the struggle forged powerful bonds of loyalty and comradeship, most obviously among the crews of the U-boats, but also in the warships escorting the convoys, whose crews were mostly composed not of regular Royal Navy personnel, but drawn from seamen engaged only for the hostilities. These seamen were more self-reliant than the average naval rating, used to sailing alone or in small crews, and totally unfazed by

Routine winter conditions on the Northern convoy route to Murmansk in Northern Russia.

the worst of Atlantic storms. Kipling understood them. In his poem 'RNVR' subtitled 'Sea Constables', he wrote of their equivalents in the First World War:

> And we both abandoned our own affairs
>   And took to the dreadful seas
> I was a dealer in stocks and shares
>   And you in butter and teas
> We saw more than the nights could hide –
>   More than the waves could keep –
> And – certain faces over the side
>   Which do not go from our sleep.

The fall of France was a catastrophe for Britain and the Royal Navy, for it enabled Doenitz to establish his base of operations on the French Atlantic coast, notably at Lorient, Bordeaux and Saint-Nazaire. Doenitz naturally made the most of the chance, building underwater submarine pens covered in 20ft (6.1m) of concrete which proved impervious to the bombs launched by Allied planes (or to the efforts of the handful of commandos able to penetrate the security screens).

He thus halved the distance the U-boats required to get to their station in mid-Atlantic and eliminated the need for them to pass down the Channel or through the North Sea, where they were far more vulnerable to attack by British ships and aircraft than they were in mid-ocean. The 'killing fields' which accounted for the majority of the sinkings were in the gap inaccessible to aircraft from Newfoundland, Iceland or Northern Ireland. The occupation of France, combined with the introduction of more modern boats, produced immediate and dramatic results: between June and September 1940 the U-boats sank 274 ships for the loss of only two of their own. This gave an 'exchange rate' of over a hundred. By June 1941 over 300,000 tons were being lost monthly, even though there were only thirteen U-boats at sea at one time.

Then the British started a series of counter-measures which, however inadequate they seemed at the time, were to result in the turn of the tide two years later. Convoys were routed further north, towards Iceland, and the escort fleet was increased to 400 ships, including fifty over-age American destroyers (known as 'four-stackers' because they had four funnels) which the British had acquired in 1940 in exchange for allowing the Americans to lease bases in the West Indies.

The situation worsened in early 1942 when the Americans joined the war. Doenitz had perfected a system of concentrating his 'wolf packs' against individual convoys. By the end of the year, wrote John Keegan,

> with sinkings running at an average of 100 ships every month, building (at 7 million tons a year) not quite replacing the 7.75 million tons sunk that year, an exchange ratio of ten ships sunk for every U-boat lost, and U-boat numbers rising absolutely through replacements from the shipyards, Doenitz was able to sense that the crisis of the Battle of the Atlantic was at hand.

At first he seemed to be winning. Two British convoys, code-named HX229 and SC122, which sailed in spring 1943 suffered terrible damage, to considerable German rejoicing. It was premature: in May three German U-boat packs totalling sixty boats attacked a single westbound British convoy. Seven U-boats were lost in a single night, and although twelve merchant ships had been lost, the 'exchange ratio' had clearly turned decisively against the Germans. By the summer the tide of war itself had swung towards the British and Americans.

The battle for the Atlantic had been 'won' in the sense that the Germans suffered heavier losses than the Allies and the number of U-boats and, even more important, their crews were steadily diminishing, though casualties continued right up until May 1945. The reasons were many and various: improvements in breaking the German naval codes; increased convoy speeds, themselves due to the introduction of the faster, mass-produced Liberty ships; and the improved radar introduced in early 1943 required to counter the U-boats' ever-developing capacity to detect airborne radar emissions. But the key to final success was the relative handful of small aircraft that could be launched from hastily improvised small carriers, and above all the Liberator bomber, which was able to operate at far longer ranges than its predecessors. By the end of the war 288 U-boats had been sunk by aircraft compared with 246 by surface craft.

Yet, for all the final success of air power (which was the equivalent in terms of important innovations in military technology of the tank in the First World War), the brunt was borne by the 'poor bloody infantry' – the merchant men and the wide variety of escort vessels. Heavy cruisers with 8in (20.3cm) guns were ineffective against surface raiders. The lighter ones, mounting only 6in (15.24cm) guns were, in theory, used as fleet support, although they easily outgunned their German equivalents, which depended on ultra-rapid fire from their lighter 4.1in (10.5cm) versions. Unfortunately, the British were ill equipped with such cruisers, for a variety of historical reasons. The *Dreadnought*-fixated 'Jackie' Fisher had originally built only 'scouts', which were simply inadequate, but before the First World War the navy had been properly equipped with cruisers mounting 4in (10.2cm) and 6in guns, including the Arethusa class of 'light armoured cruisers' powered by destroyer-type turbines, which were uncomfortable but easy to improve and expand.

Design between the wars was dogged by a number of disarmament agreements – as we have seen, the Washington Treaty of 1921 led to the scrapping of many of the navy's best cruisers and called a halt to any building programmes – as well as stupidity, which resulted in the County class, disasters with a tremendous freeboard of nearly 30ft (9.2m) which might have made them look aggressive, but which were outdated in design and rightly nicknamed 'tinclads'. The London Treaty of 1930 further impeded the designers by laying down grossly inadequate limits in size and number of cruisers. As Sydney Poole says, 'By 1935 just thirty-two modern ones . . . were available, all unequal in one way or another to any foreign vessels built since the Great War, and the unpalatable fact had to be accepted that the navy was no longer able to protect the country's seaborne commerce.' The situation was exacerbated by the fact that only England had agreed to limit her total construction of cruisers for the next six years to a measly 91,000 tons and had accepted a total cruiser fleet of a mere fifty.

Inevitably, therefore, on the outbreak of the Second World War Britain had to rely on the handful of cruisers built at the end of the first conflict and between the wars – such as the Ceres or Cardiff class, of a mere 4,200 tons – along with the last of the small light cruisers, the barely bigger D class, built in the early 1920s and the County class, weighing nearly 10,000 tons, which managed to slip through the disarmament net in the 1920s. The late 1930s saw a building programme whose results included the Towns, capable of 32 knots and carrying twelve 6in guns. To speed up rearmament the Admiralty also commissioned a dozen cruisers within the 8,000-ton treaty limit. These proved, quite literally, life-savers (although Churchill referred to them patronizingly as the 'poor little Fijis'), but the fact remains that throughout the war the British suffered from a lack of cruisers, and from what they did have being a scratch lot.

The Fijis were used in two distinct roles: in convoys against U-boats they were the kings of the seas, but as a screen protecting bigger ships they were helpless. Typically, two cruisers, *Cornwall* and *Dorsetshire*, acting as pawns against the marauding Japanese in the Indian Ocean in April 1942, were both soon sunk. However, they had distracted the enemy long enough to allow the main fleet to escape and to lure the Japanese to within range of shore-based aircraft from Ceylon. More positively, *Sheffield* and *Norfolk* protected a helpless convoy against the German pocket battleship *Scharnhorst* before the battleship *Duke of York* arrived to finish her off. Kipling understood their self-sacrificing role. In his poem 'Cruiser' he wrote:

> For this is our office – to spy and make room,
> As hiding yet guiding the foe to their doom;
> Surrounding, confounding, we bait and betray
> And tempt them to battle the sea's width away.

If only because they were more numerous, destroyers were even more valuable as convoy escorts. For all the usual reasons Britain never had enough of them and, for the first years of the war, anyway, had to rely on the sturdy old V and

W classes, partly because newer designs like the Tribal class could only be built in relatively small numbers because of their size and complexity. The Vs and Ws were a link with the days of large flotillas and Dreadnought battle squadrons. They had been designed in a hurry amid the sound and fury of the First World War, two prototypes being launched within a year of the first order. The W class was originally a private venture by John Thornycroft, a heavier improvement on the V class, with up to six 4in guns, all carried high above the waterline in defiance of the whole of the previous canon of destroyer design. As Anthony Preston points out, 'the youngest of them was fifteen years old in 1939 and the oldest had been laid down twenty-three years before.'[7] Yet 'these veterans of the Kaiser's war saw some of the most arduous service imaginable'. Unusually among British warships, they were also superior to the German equivalents, which were top-heavy because of their over-ambitious armament.

Notwithstanding the haste with which they were produced and the departure from established design, the Vs and Ws combined all the best and most advanced features of destroyers of their time, and as Preston says, 'every destroyer afloat today owes something in layout to them'. They were capable of 30 knots and, with a boiler removed, could cross the Atlantic without refuelling. They were excellent in close support because they were fast and manoeuvrable, but they were wet above decks and violent in motion. And because they were intended to carry heavy guns and torpedos they were difficult to adapt to take anti-torpedo weapons. In addition, they were fitted with adequate heating and insulation only when they went in for major refits.

Their finest hour was probably during Operation Dynamo, the evacuation from Dunkirk and other northern French ports at the end of May 1940. Carrying up to 1,300 men at a time, they were pressed into service to help to rescue far more than the 10,000 men a day foreseen in the first evacuation plans, which were drawn up as late as 20 May. Six of the class were damaged and one was sunk, and by the end of the evacuation the navy had only seventy-four destroyers left undamaged.

In the Atlantic escorts sailed in groups, usually comprising three destroyers and six other ships, including armed trawlers, corvettes and frigates. Because Asdic (later known as sonar), the key underwater detection and ranging apparatus devised in 1918 by a Canadian scientist, could not be used at above 20 knots, the most desperate requirement was for smaller seaworthy vessels operating below that speed. This prompted the development of new craft, including the Bitterns, the only sloop of the 1930s which provided effective fire against both aircraft and submarines. The Bitterns begat the Egrets, and they in turn the 1,340-ton Black Swans with their quadruple 2lb (0.91kg) anti-aircraft mounting. But as H.T. Lenton says: 'Although eminently suitable for escort work, the Black Swan class as a whole was too complex to meet the very heavy demand for escort vessels and the bulk of escort work consequently fell on the more numerous corvettes and frigates.'

The standby throughout the war was the Flower class of corvettes, or 'convoy sloops', as they were officially known until 1937. In 1939 Smiths Docks had submitted a sketch plan for a coastal escort based on their whaler *Southern Pride* (a ship based on a trawler would not have been capable of the 16 knots required by the Admiralty). In the next three years 300 Flower-class corvettes were ordered from Canadian as well as British shipyards. After the fall of France they were pressed into convoy duty in mid-ocean, for which they had not been designed. In 1940 they were modified to provide more accommodation, but, as Lenton explains in a notable piece of understatement:

> From their inception the Flower class was recognized as an extremely crude means of taking into action an Asdic set, depth charges and a 4in gun . . . not unnaturally, they did not provide ideal ocean escorts as they were too short for the task, and while good sea boats they were too lively in adverse conditions to the extent that crew efficiency was impaired.[8]

The face of modern shipbuilding. Three type 23 frigates on the stocks at Yarrow's yard on the Clyde.

Nevertheless, 'During the critical years between 1940 and 1943 they were the only type of escort available, and were kept actively employed right up to the end of hostilities.' The U-boats were not to know that the Asdic 'pinging' on them came from a fleet destroyer or a small, slow, lightly-armed escort vessel.

Only later were the corvettes reinforced by the bigger, faster, more suitable River class. The difference was signalled by the description of the River-class vessels as frigates, their twin screws (the Flowers had only a single screw) and two sets of corvette machinery giving 20 knots. Frigate was an old term – Nelson, who relied on them as his eyes and ears in the days before radar, was everlastingly complaining that he didn't have enough of them – but in the Second World War they were reborn in a new form, as fast as a destroyer and carrying the armaments of the smaller corvette. The new-style frigate could average 20 knots, cross the Atlantic without refuelling, deploy a full battery of underwater weapons including forward-firing depth-charge-launchers, and could accommodate a crew of 100 in reasonable comfort. The classic design were the seventy-eight ships in the Captain class, designed to be built in the United States and thus equipped with American diesel engines.

The Battle of the Atlantic was the last naval battle fought primarily by ships. It was no coincidence that the biggest ships built for the US Navy after the war were aircraft-carriers, starting with the USS *Forrestal*, an 86,000-tonner launched in 1954. Even in that classic amphibious operation the Falklands War, the Royal Navy was largely confined to the roles of escort, aircraft-carrier and troop-carrier.

Throughout the campaign it was clear that the loss of even a ship as big as the type 42 destroyer HMS *Sheffield* was not of crucial importance, whereas if either of the two aircraft-carriers had been hit, then the outcome of the battle would have been in doubt.

The primary symbol of the navy in recent years has been not aircraft-carriers but its handful of nuclear-powered submarines, armed with either torpedos or atomic missiles. The Falklands War was an exception. Today's – and tomorrow's – wars are clearly going to be small, messy affairs, typically offshore, peace-keeping operations requiring large numbers of smaller, more flexible vessels. Remember Nelson's eternal complaints that he never had enough frigates.

Unfortunately, the politically-inspired decision to concentrate on useless and hideously expensive nuclear-powered submarines has greatly reduced the actual – and still more the future – effectiveness of the Royal Navy, which nonetheless remains the world's most successful instrument of warfare at sea. Whether its confusion and reputation can survive the present debilitating defence policy is another matter.

IN 1871, in a private initiative, Messrs Thornycroft built *Miranda*, the Royal Navy's first fast-attack boat, which logged a speed of 16.4 knots. It was successful enough to be sold to a dozen European navies. Six years later the Admiralty ordered one, called *Lightning*. Then in 1894 came *Turbinia*, and a host of racing machines developed throughout Europe. In 1906 Thornycroft built the flat-bottomed *Dragonfly* for the navy. With its flat-bottomed hull, it hydroplaned over the water and created far less drag than its predecessors. It became the standard coastal motor boat (CMB) used by the navy in the First World War.

The navy abandoned fast-attack craft in 1926 – just at the wrong moment, but again a private initiative came to the rescue. In the late 1920s Hubert ('Scotty') Scott-Paine of Supermarine Aviation started to apply aeronautical techniques to the design of fast motorboats, in particular to a revolutionary new shape of hull, the 'hard chine', based on his work on flying boats – two gentle curves each side of a pointed keel. 'Scotty' used racing boats such as *Miss England* and *Miss Britain* to promote ideas like RAF 206, an air–sea rescue launch he produced in 1931. It was tested to its limits by Aircraftsman T.E. Shaw (better known as Lawrence of Arabia), who is remembered by one contemporary, eighty-five-year-old Harry Banks, as a 'total speed freak'.

The navy distrusted Scotty's brash commercialism, so they took up a similar design developed by his arch-rivals, Vosper's. The result was the MTB 102. These were appallingly vulnerable, and in any case could not put out to sea in anything approaching heavy weather. They would sneak up on their targets like submarines and fire their torpedos, relying on speed and manoeuvrability. The Admiralty placed a low priority on fast MTBs, and one result was that they lacked reliable engines.

The 102 was originally designed to accommodate the Italian Isotta-Fraschinis, but the Admiralty would not give the firm a big enough order, maintaining that the vessels should be powered by Rolls-Royce Merlin engines. Unfortunately, these were all required for fighter planes and the MTBs had to make do with anything they could get.

Even the reliable Packard V12s they acquired after 1942 did not match the boats, and the resulting 'lash-up' meant that one out of four boats would fail on every mission. Not surprisingly, only two of the twenty-two sub-lieutenants who signed up for MTBs in 1939 survived the war – the navy treated the ships and their crews as far more expendable than larger craft. But they did their job: while British coastal convoys ran almost uninterrupted throughout the war, the Germans' convoys along the French and Dutch coasts were severely restricted and almost stopped altogether.

By the end of the Second World War the British had proper motor torpedo boats, like this example of a type 521.

THE GREAT LINERS – AND SOME LESSER ONES AS WELL

LTHOUGH STEAM POWER became a practical proposition in the second quarter of the nineteenth century, the 'great liner' did not emerge immediately. For several decades the fuel-hungry paddle wheel limited its range and confined its role to carrying high-value freight. In the 1830s and 1840s, designers managed to reduce the previous uneconomic consumption levels, but it took the genius of Isambard Kingdom Brunel, creator of the Great Western Railway, to accelerate the development of the modern liner. His first effort was the *Great Western*, an integral part of his dream of providing a regular steam-powered service between London and New York using steamships to cross the Atlantic. The *Great Western* was the only liner serving New York. His rival Samuel Cunard, himself a Canadian by birth, centred his operation on the port of Halifax in eastern Canada. Even so, the *Great Western* was an uneconomic proposition: despite its extremely sophisticated engineering (and its equally highly developed auxiliary sails), it still had to rely on paddle wheels.

Brunel made quite astonishing strides in the evolution of the liner in the course of building one ship, the *Great Britain*. When it was laid down in 1838 he planned to build a wooden paddle-steamer. A year later he ordered an iron keel and the next year he cancelled the order for paddles and placed one for a screw propeller, a six-bladed effort

15ft 6in (4.72m) in diameter, and of amazingly modern design. Inevitably, the design changes delayed the launch until 1845. The commercial world soon followed him in using iron. The only constraint was the need to obtain government approval: the shipping lines all depended on mail contracts and the Admiralty, which had to give its approval, was loth to abandon its 'hearts of oak' until the mid-1850s. The screw propeller took longer to catch on because low-pressure engines did not provide sufficient power to drive it, except at an exorbitant cost in coal.

Despite its high fuel consumption, *Great Britain* proved its worth on the Australian run, where it lasted until 1876. It was eventually abandoned on the Falkland Islands, where it served as a coal bunker until it was rescued in the 1960s, restored several years later and, as was only appropriate, found a permanent home in Bristol. But Brunel was always pursued by some inner demon which led him to go too far: the result was the ill-fated *Great Eastern*, which, at 32,000 tons, was six times the size of any other ship afloat, a record it held for the incredible period of forty years. It was its size that was the problem: it was too big to be propelled purely by screw propellers, and they had to be supplemented by uneconomic paddle wheels. In that respect at least, it was a step back from the *Great Britain*.

Truly the height of luxury: the first class dining room on the *Normandie*, a triumph of art-deco design and the finest liner of its day. Sadly it was destroyed by fire in New York Harbor in 1941.

Brunel's *Great Western* leaving for its maiden voyage across the Atlantic in 1838. Brunel proved that a paddle-steamer could provide a regular Atlantic service, albeit at an uneconomically high cost in fuel.

The problem of providing sufficient power for the screw propeller was not solved until the 1860s. A Scottish engineer, James Elder, had developed a compound engine which used steam far more effectively by splitting the expansion of the steam, which provided the power, between two (or, as soon became more usual, three) cylinders. This arrangement also reduced the range of temperatures in the engine and provided more torque. It also increased the possible steam pressure, thus further improving efficiency. In the 1880s steam boilers reached what was effectively their final form when iron was replaced by steel from the new-fangled Bessemer blast furnaces. Steel was so much stronger than iron that boiler pressures could be multiplied several times to well over 100lb per sq in. It was the development of the high-pressure triple-expansion engine (i.e., one with three cylinders) rather than the usual explanation – the opening of the Suez Canal in 1869, shortening the sea route to the East – that resulted in the golden age of passenger liners.

The switch from paddle to propeller power set off a race for speed, glamour and comfort which was to last for nearly a century. The liner companies were always quick to seize on any new technology, and once the potential of the steam turbine had been so dramatically demonstrated by Charles Parsons at the 1897 Spithead Review (see page 22) they started to apply it. The new technology offered a most precious advantage: smaller bulk leading to greater room for passengers and cargo. By 1905 the Allan line had launched the 10,600-ton turbine-powered *Virginian* and *Victorian* into service on the north Atlantic run, and Cunard was adding a new engine to the *Carmania*, a 19,500-tonner then under construction on the Clyde. The turbines were as big as possible to help reduce shaft revolutions and thus increase the efficiency of the propellers. In all, over a million blades were required.

The early turbines installed in the *Carmania* consumed far more fuel than the equivalent reciprocating engines installed in its twin, the *Caronia* (this popular pair of ships were known as the 'Pretty Sisters'). Nevertheless, Cunard switched to turbines for its next major investments, the *Lusitania* and the *Mauretania*. These vessels were the result of a series of scientific studies of hull form, which involved far more detailed instructions from Cunard than had previously been usual (Harland & Wolff, a pioneering yard in Belfast, had been especially famous for its independence in designing new liners). The two ships, at 32,000 tons apiece, were too big for a number of yards. They also required six turbines: two high-pressure ones whose exhaust was channelled into four of low pressure, which provided the power directly to the four propellers.

As far as liners were concerned, the gradual change from coal to oil which took until the 1920s to complete was of equal if not greater importance than the switch to turbines. Coal not only occupied a disproportionate share of hull space, but it involved employing literally hundreds of stokers, for whom accommodation (of a sort) had to be provided. The *Lusitania*, for instance, consumed 1,000 tons of coal daily on the Atlantic run, an appetite which required 400 stokers. The change also spared passengers on long routes the tedium of waiting for days at coaling ports for the boat to be refuelled by hand, and greatly reduced the grime inevitably spread by any form of coal-fired boiler. Indeed, until the development of steam-powered loading equipment in the 1880s, the process was so dirty that passengers at ports like Aden were advised to disembark while the ship was taking on coal.

Overleaf: By 1934 the twenty-seven-year-old *Mauretania* had earned the right to the title 'grand old lady of the Atlantic'. It was in danger of being scrapped but was sufficiently appreciated to be refitted just after this photograph was taken.

Below: The launch of Brunel's *Great Britain* in Bristol on 19 July 1843, a much more advanced vessel than the one laid down five years earlier.

After 1918 Britain began to lag in technical developments. The P & O company was typical in remaining technically conservative. Its major innovation in the 1930s was to adopt the use of electric transmission combined with orthodox turbines. This idea, which allowed ships to proceed full speed astern as well as ahead, was first developed in the United States. A natural corollary of this general cautiousness was that British ship owners proved slower than their European counterparts to adopt diesel engines, which provided all the advantages of compactness and smaller crews they were looking for, although they were not suitable for the biggest liners. Only Sir Owen Philipps, later Lord Kylsant, of the Royal Mail group, which included Union Castle and the White Star line among its subsidiaries, committed himself wholeheartedly to the new engine. In the event, until after 1945 anyway, diesel propulsion proved most suitable for smaller vessels steaming at below 20 knots. Even then British owners had to continue to rely on turbines, since they did not have access to large diesels like the 35,000bhp Fiat engines installed by the Italians in two ships designed for the service from Genoa to the River Plate.

The size and position of the engine and its associated fuel supply was of prime importance in determining the design and spaciousness of passenger accommodation, and it was not until the construction of the Southern Cross after the war (see the feature on page 47) that naval architects adopted the obvious solution: to put the engines aft and thus to give the passengers free run over the entire forward two-thirds of the ship. Previously, the accommodation was arranged in a more or less standard format. As Robert Gardiner and Ambrose Greenway described it: 'The first-class cabins/staterooms and their social rooms were grouped amidships, the exception being the dining room, which was normally placed lower and further forward. Those for the second class were generally one or two decks lower and extended from just aft of amidships to just beyond the mainmast.'[1] Needless to say, passengers in third class (or steerage) were in the very bowels of the ship, which emphasized their lowly status in the pecking order.

I
N 1955 HARLAND AND WOLFF built a revolutionary liner, the 20,000-ton *Southern Cross*. Although it was designed for a relatively unglamorous route, Shaw Savill's round-the-world service via South Africa and the Panama Canal, the designers took a step so obvious that it is a wonder that no one had ever thought of it before: they placed the engines – and the single, smallish, streamlined, funnel – aft, thus providing passengers with an unrestricted run of the rest of the ship. The space was unencumbered by cargo, since the *Southern Cross* was designed for passengers only, and thus avoided the port delays inevitable with cargo liners.

The promenade deck stretched virtually the whole 600ft (182.88m) length of the ship and served as the base for the superstructure. The saloon decks had two restaurants, which between them covered the full width of the ship, and two swimming pools, one high on the forward end of the sun deck. The 1,160 passengers were all housed in tourist class, another innovation. The layout also permitted a 'lounge' deck with a magnificent forward-facing room flanked by such amenities as a cinema, a taverna and a writing room-cum-library.

Sensibly, Shaw Savill had planned to use the ship for both regular traffic and holiday-makers. The design was so successful that in 1961 the company introduced a second very similar ship, the *Northern Star*. Between them *Southern Cross* and *Northern Star* provided eight round-the-world services every year, conveying roughly the same number of passengers as it had taken the eleven vessels in the line's fleet to carry in 1939. As so often in transport history – as indeed was the case with steam engines and propeller-driven aircraft – the last examples of a soon-to-be-outdated technique were the finest specimens of their kind.

Shaw Savill's *Southern Cross*. As late as 1955 its clear sweeping decks were still an attractive novelty.

Even for the first and second classes, accommodation was generally far less luxurious than that offered by the handful of staterooms featured in the companies' advertisements. The cabins were purely functional, and in most cases passengers had to cross a passage to get to the bathroom or lavatory. Before the First World War an ensuite bathroom was a luxury, and even after the Second World War many liners were built without them. But during the first half of the twentieth century liners were transformed from mere methods of transport to providers of what might nowadays be called a 'cruise experience' during, say, the five days of an Atlantic crossing or the six weeks required to sail to New Zealand. There were exceptions: the Royal Mail line in particular felt that the passengers should be segregated from the officers, and the latter had the sole run of a massive bridge deck, but this was a rare deviation from the concept that a sea journey should be a pleasure (except, of course, for the immigrants and other unfortunates battened down below in steerage).

As early as 1889 one W.J. Loftie could assert that: 'The rush and worry of modern life has promoted the creation of luxurious floating hotels on the sea . . . excellent for the health of the healthy as well as invalids.'[2] Loftie gave a long list of sporting activities – cricket, tennis, quoits, curling, bowls, hopscotch and gymnastics – made possible largely because the installation of the more compact compound expansion engines left the decks free of coal. Such exercise was necessary to combat the effects of the many hearty meals which were another feature of life aboard luxury liners throughout their reign. As a result of their new role as floating health resorts, liners were equipped with an increasing number of facilities – the interior swimming pools, for example, which were designed to supplement the much more casual open-air affairs that originally consisted of a temporary canvas erection slung on deck. Probably the first liner to boast a Turkish bath (as well as squash courts) was the *Olympic*, the biggest liner in the world when it was built a few years before the First World War. During the health-conscious 1920s a gymnasium became a standard fitment and sometimes first-class passengers had the use of a

couple of tennis courts. Every liner worthy of the name had its own hairdressers, a shop and other features whose remnants can be seen on ferries, the only contact most modern travellers have with sea travel.

Until the 1880s passenger comfort was limited because ships were lit only by candles and oil lamps. The White Star's *Adriatic* and *Celtic*, built for the north Atlantic trade in 1872, were originally equipped with lighting fired by coal gas, but frequent fractures caused by the movement of the hull soon put paid to that system. So the companies were naturally quick to seize on the advantages offered by electric power. As early as 1879 the Inman liner *City of Berlin* was equipped with a few arc lamps, but it was the development that year of the incandescent filament lamp that set off a revolution. Within four years electric lights were being specified for all new vessels, and at the turn of the century the introduction of electrically driven ventilation fans marked a major step forward and led to the use of electricity throughout ships, in the galleys and auxiliary plant as well as in the passenger accommodation.

Air conditioning spread slowly from a few favoured staterooms to the lesser accommodation in the 1950s, but even liners like the 17,000-ton *Kenya Castle*, built in 1951 for Union–Castle's round-Africa service, relied on mechanical ventilation and punkah louvres. Stability, first achieved by the elaborate system fitted to the great Italian liner *Conte di Savoia* in 1932, became the norm only after the development of the Denny–Brown stabilizer, the device which stopped the *Queen Mary* from rolling so badly after it was fitted to her in 1958.

The public rooms of the great Atlantic liners were naturally showcases for the very latest in fashionable decor. Undoubtedly the finest was that magnificent French liner the *Normandie*, which broke all existing records on its maiden voyage in May 1935. Its art-deco interiors were miles removed from what John M. Maber calls the 'plastic and chrome decoration of contemporary German liners, or the baroque interiors of the Italian liners *Rex* and *Conte di Savoia*'.[3] Few of the liners had a properly co-ordinated interior design, though the Orient line's *Orion*, launched in 1935, was another notable exception.

The balance between passengers and cargo was different on virtually every major run. (So was the type of cargo: the services between England and South Africa, for example, were based on mail.) Moreover, the type of accommodation provided on the Atlantic run changed dramatically in the early 1920s, when the Americans shut their doors to the immigrants who had formed a staple of the trade. The removal of steerage class, which had accommodated the vast majority of immigrants (and very few other passengers) merely emphasized the primacy of the Atlantic run. It was the first to provide a regular service; it was more glamorous; its customers represented an assured and ever-growing traffic. The service had to be regular and punctual (not for nothing was it called the Atlantic ferry) and so required the fastest, latest ships, all of which competed for the notional

Blue Riband awarded to the liner making the crossing in the shortest possible time. It was also untypical, since it was far more competitive than other services, and was seen as a race for national prestige. Not surprisingly, speed records were regularly broken. In 1869 the Inman liner *City of Brussels* took the Blue Riband from Cunard. But, as Maber says, the arrival of the newcomer 'came as a salutary reminder that prestige is ephemeral where the public whim is concerned'. *City of Brussels'* record was soon challenged by the White Star's 3,700-ton *Oceanic*, the first ship on the run to be fitted with the newly developed compound engines. White Star had left the design to Harland & Wolff, advocates of a 'long ship' – one with a length-to-beam ratio of ten rather than the more usual eight. This ratio created heavy vibration aft, where the first-class passengers had previously been accommodated, a habit inherited from the days of steam. *Oceanic* broke conclusively with that hangover

The 17,000 ton *Oceanic*, the second liner to carry the name, and the first to be easily convertible into an armed merchant cruiser.

and the best cabins (and the first-class saloon) were sited amidships and outclassed the competition from Cunard.

White Star's 5,000-ton *Britannic* and *Germanic*, built by Harland & Wolff in the 1870s, set a new standard, although they retained auxiliary sail power. Indeed the *Germanic* survived until 1950, for the last few years of its life under Turkish ownership. The Cunarder *Parthia*, built in 1870, lasted almost as long, crossing the Atlantic and the Pacific and spending its final years on the American Pacific coast before it was at last withdrawn from service in 1952.

The battle hotted up with the growth of the International Mercantile Marine Co., organized by the great American financier J. Pierpoint Morgan, who tried to achieve the sort of monopoly on the Atlantic run that he had already enjoyed in many of America's basic industries, such as steel. He was foiled only by the refusal of Cunard to become involved with him. After the construction of the *Teutonic* in 1889, White Star, controlled by Morgan at the time (he later

Guess what? Yes, it's the Titanic *striking an iceberg, the most publicised accident in maritime history.*

sold it to Philipps) abandoned the idea of going for records, preferring to rely instead on the appeal of ships like the 21,000-ton *Celtic* which were both comfortable and economic to operate, a combination designed to attract travellers and make a profit at the same time.

White Star's 17,000-tonner, another *Oceanic*, was the first North Atlantic liner to be built for rapid conversion to act as an armed merchant cruiser, a role which provided a number of governments with an excuse for subsidizing their countries' ships. Such support was not new: in the late 1850s the British government had bought the *Himalaya*, an early P & O propeller-driven steamship, after it had served in the Crimean War as a troopship (much to the relief of the owners, who had found the vessel hopelessly uneconomic). But in the early years of the twentieth century subsidies became the norm: the beautiful 45,500-ton *Aquitania*, completed in 1914, immediately went into service as an armed merchant carrier, hospital ship and troopship, while in the Second World War the 'Queens' were famous for their ability to whisk up to 15,000 troops across the Atlantic at over 30 knots. The record subsidy was paid by the American government, which spent nearly $70 million on building the *United States*. The ship captured the Blue Riband in 1952, establishing a record which is unlikely ever to be beaten. The ship was then 'sold' to United States Lines for a paltry $32 million.

The international race for supremacy on the Atlantic reached its peak in the twenty-five years before the outbreak of war in 1914. The pace of progress was so fast that when the *Oceanic* went into service in 1899, White Star's other vessels, the *Majestic* and the *Teutonic*, were considered past their prime, even though they were only nine and ten years old respectively. Cunard's *Campania* and *Lucania*, both 13,000-tonners built in 1893, were soon outclassed by more modern German ships, but in 1907 Cunard introduced two magnificent new liners, the *Lusitania* and *Mauretania*. The *Lusitania* was sunk by a U-boat in the first months of the First World War, but the *Mauretania*, its 32,000 tons propelled by four direct-drive steam turbines, held the Blue Riband until 1929, an eternity in the history of Atlantic travel. The 46,000-ton

Queen Mary, the dream: as portrayed by Charles Pears when she arrived at Southampton on 27 March 1936 after her maiden voyage.

Aquitania, the third ship of the trio required to maintain a weekly service from Liverpool to New York, was slower but immensely popular because of its superior stability. It sailed an estimated 1.3 million miles (2.1 million km) before being towed to the breakers' yard in 1950.

The White Star line attempted to compete by providing a fast weekly service using its own three new liners. Unfortunately for the company, its efforts were a disaster. Of the three only the *Olympic* survived for any length of time. The *Britannic* was commissioned as a hospital ship late in 1915 and was sunk less than a year later, while the fate of the third, the *Titanic*, is too well known to require retelling here.

In the late 1920s Cunard's older ships were overshadowed by French and above all German newcomers – the German *Bremen* captured the Blue Riband in 1929. The next year Cunard announced that it would build two new superliners to outdo the foreign competition. However, the first, the *Queen Mary*, lay, an empty hulk, in dock for five years after it was laid down in 1930. The delay was due to the severity of the Depression, which also resulted in a

merger between Cunard and its historic rival, White Star, in 1934, an arrangement hastened by the fact that White Star's chairman, Lord Kylsant, had just featured in one of the most sensational fraud trials of the century. The next year the British government advanced £3 million so that the *Queen Mary* could be completed and a further £5 million for a sister ship, the *Queen Elizabeth*. The *Mary* – not an advanced design, since it was in many ways simply a larger, faster, updated version of the *Aquitania* – soon snatched back the Blue Riband, crossing the Atlantic in only four days (and thirty minutes).

Most of the other, longer, routes connected the Imperial powers – principally Britain and France – with their colonies, and naturally they enjoyed overwhelming advantages. This did not stop the ambitious French company Messageries Maritimes from competing east of Suez, as did the heavily subsidized ships of the German Nord-Deutscher Lloyd line in the 1890s. They had taken advantage of the fact that the dominant company, P & O, had been caught completely unawares by the opening of the Suez Canal in 1869. P & O hastily ordered the *Khedive*, its first iron-built, screw-propelled steamer, and continued with the *Australia*, the last of the company's barque-rigged, clipper-stemmed steamers. But the *Australia* – and successors like the *Rohilla* – were completely outclassed by the Orient line's *Austral*, a 16-knot, steel-hulled vessel built in 1881 which offered a far higher standard of accommodation as well as the ventilation so essential on the run from Suez down the Red Sea to Bombay.

Another major 'imperial' route was to South Africa and centred round the mail contract – hence the famous regularity of the service, which departed every Friday at 4 p.m. from Southampton. In the 1860s the Union Steamship company set the record when its 2,000-ton *Danube* covered the 5,970 miles (9,318km) from Southampton to Table Bay in under twenty-six days. In the 1870s the Castle Mail Packets Company fought back with ships like the *Dunrobin Castle*, which, with a service speed of 12 to 14 knots, could reach the Cape in twenty-one and a half days. The battle

between the two firms for supremacy was interrupted by a short slump until gold was discovered in the Witswatersrand in 1885, generating a market for the transport of thousands of emigrants.

It was Castle, the newcomer, which felt it had to set the pace in a manner typical of new entrants challenging more sober, better-established companies (like Cunard on the north Atlantic and P & O east of Suez). But Union fought back effectively with the *Norman* (built by Harland and Wolff in Belfast, like most of the forward-looking ships of the time). With triple-expansion machinery driving twin screws, a service speed of 16 knots and accommodation superior to anything bar the stars of the north Atlantic, it set a standard for the next fifteen years. Special design was also required

Opposite: *Queen Mary,* the reality: sailing for New York from Southampton in April 1948. But it was still luxurious enough to be the object of longing for Brits still subject to postwar austerity and food rationing.

Below: *Oriana,* one of the two luxury liners commissioned by P & O just as aircraft were taking over, and thus condemned to spend its entire life cruising.

for another canal, the Panama, the passage to the South Seas. Typical were the three motor liners (*Rangitiki, Rangitane* and *Rangitoto*) built on the Clyde in the late 1920s for the New Zealand Shipping Company, elegant ships of 17,000 tons designed to carry a heavy load of cargo as well as 600 passengers.

Until the 1950s ship owners were still looking forward to future success, even though they were tending to buy smaller, more flexible vessels. As Maber points out, in the summer of 1950 Cunard White Star 'was employing no fewer than nine vessels in the New York trade alone, in additon to four working out from Southampton to Canadian ports'. But the arrival of the jet-propelled air liner in the late 1950s spelled doom for the great liners. The figures tell the story with stark simplicity: in 1957 a record 1,036,000 passengers crossed the Atlantic by sea; the next year, when the Boeing 707 entered service, it carried more passengers than all the great liners combined. In 1960 nearly 2 million passengers crossed the Atlantic by air, over twice as many as went by sea, and within five years regular services had virtually ceased. Even the finest and most modern liners were immediately and inevitably diverted from scheduled services to cruising (or even more mundane occupations: two flagships of the former Italian fleet were reduced to dormitory ships in the Persian Gulf), while the *Queen Mary* was demoted to a floating hotel and conference centre, like a wild animal tethered in a circus ring.

But it is a more modest ship, the *Leicestershire*, which is perhaps the perfect example of this lost world, precisely because it was never a glamorous vessel. A 9,000-tonner, it was built on the Clyde in 1949 to serve Bibby line's long-established 'colonial' service between Liverpool, Colombo and Rangoon. Although it was designed primarily for cargo, it could carry seventy-six passengers, all in first class, providing the customary swimming pool, hairdressers and shop. But the times were against her and in 1965 she was sold to a Greek company and converted into a car ferry, foundering three years later in a particularly violent Mediterranean storm.

The *QEII* making its stately and glamorous way into Boston harbour for repairs in 1992.

A handful of great ships had only the briefest of lives as true liners before being transformed into cruise vessels. The obvious case is the *Queen Elizabeth II*, a much smaller vessel than the original Queens. At the last minute Cunard decided to build a ship more suited to cruising than its elder sisters. Even better examples are P & O's twins, *Oriana* and *Canberra*. They are much the same size, around 45,000 tons, both cruise at 27 knots, and both entered service on the UK–Australia run in the early 1960s just as the jet was taking over. But otherwise they were total opposites: the *Oriana* had geared turbines placed amidships, the *Canberra* relied on turbo-electric power, with the engines aft. *Canberra*, of course, came into its own in the Falklands War, when, like so many of her great predecessors, she served as a troopship, attracting the highest of all accolades: a nickname. But it is unlikely that we will ever see the like of the noble 'Great White Whale' again.

The liner as war hero. The *Canberra* returning from the Falklands War after earning the affectionate sobriquet of the 'Great White Whale'.

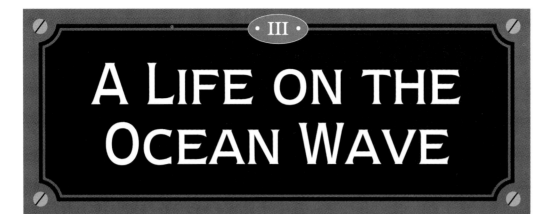

A LIFE ON THE OCEAN WAVE

THE HISTORY OF MERCHANT SHIPS is a double story, industrial and human. The industrial side tells of the advent and gradual improvement of the steam-powered ocean-going merchant ship over the past century and a quarter and the development of specialist types of vessel. Since 1960 this has led to a dual revolution: the replacement of virtually every other type of cargo carrier by the container ship and the quantum leap in the size of oil-carriers – and, to a lesser extent, other bulk ships. The second story, properly told, would take up whole volumes. It tells of the men working the ships, a life that, for all its superficial appeal, was and remains almost invariably hard, lonely, dangerous, and deeply unglamorous.

The advent of the steamship and the death of the sailing merchant ship were both more prolonged than is generally imagined. It was not until the late nineteenth century that steam, first introduced eighty years earlier, finally triumphed. Large-scale construction of merchant sailing ships, particularly the schooners which required far fewer hands than other designs, did not cease until the 1890s, and these vessels continued to serve for forty further years. The First World War saw a last burst of construction and a few merchant sailing ships were built after the war in the Aaland Islands off Sweden. The last British-registered square-rigged ship, the *William Mitchell*, was broken up in 1927 and the

forces of sail were only finally defeated by the slump of the 1930s, although the three-masted *Frederick P. Elkin* carried coal from Newport News in Virginia to Barbados in 1947 and a few survived even longer in the Indian Ocean. Ironically, their life was prolonged by their replacements, the coal-fired steamships, because these required stocks of coal at every port the world over, however tiny and inaccessible. And sailing ships were ideal carriers of cargos like coal where economy was a more important factor than speed of delivery.

Ocean-going steamships were the exception until the 1860s, when the opening of the Suez Canal greatly reduced the number of coaling stations required. But, as we saw in Chapter 2, it was a Scottish engineer, John Elder, who set the steamboat rolling through the development of the compound steam engine. The first ship he built was the *Brandon*, a coaster which used 30 per cent less fuel than its simpler predecessors. His efforts led to the construction of the Fairfield Shipyard at Govan, one of the few British yards to survive the industrial blitz unleashed by Mrs Thatcher's financial Luftwaffe.

Elder's triumph was carried a step further forward by an enterprising ship owner, Alfred Holt. In 1865 he ordered three vessels with compound engines which could carry 3,000-ton loads at 10 knots over 8,500 miles (13,679km) at a

Boats unloading between London Bridge and Tower Bridge in the days before 1939 when the Thames really was a working river.

stretch. Holt immediately introduced them in the China trade, cutting weeks off the time previously taken by even the fastest clippers, and from then on the sailing ship was, effectively, doomed. But steam's final success came only in the 1880s, when steel at last replaced iron thanks to the ability of the newly developed Bessemer furnaces to supply the world's needs. Steel was strong enough to withstand far higher boiler pressures than iron. The pioneer was the *Aberdeen*, whose triple-expansion engine, working at 125lb per sq in, took it from London to Melbourne in a mere forty-two days in 1881. As efficiency increased, so, in the words of Basil Greenhill, 'A first-class cargo steamer of the late years of Queen Victoria's reign could carry 1 ton of cargo 1 mile [1.6km] using heat in her furnace equivalent to that generated by burning one sheet of high quality Victorian writing paper.'[1]

Like the Maxim machine-gun, the triple-expansion compound steam engine was an important industrial advance which happened to serve British imperial ambitions. In the years when it was introduced the British sway over the world's oceans seemed complete. The Americans, their biggest rivals, found their expansionary instincts – and their manufacturing facilities – fully occupied in settling and satisfying the limitless demands offered by the Americans' drive westwards across their continent.

In the 1920s the geared turbine started to replace the reciprocating engine, albeit only for the faster vessels, but the end of British supremacy was already foreseeable: foreign owners, above all the Scandinavians, took to diesel engines well before their British counterparts, although some pioneers, such as Andrew Weir's Bank line, started to equip their ships with diesels later in the decade. The majority were worried about a possible lack of bunker fuel and unexpected rises in price. But diesels, though they cost more to build, provided far greater flexibility than steam. Lower fuel consumption meant a longer range, and the fuel could be stored in double-bottomed tanks which, unlike the bunkers used for coal, did not impinge on valuable cargo space. And of course diesels required even fewer hands in the engine room than a coal-fired ship, even one fitted with mechanical stoking equipment. In the 1930s, however, the development of compact, relatively low-cost diesels by Doxford's of Sunderland encouraged most British owners to make the change, albeit only for new tonnage.

The drift away from British ownership between the wars was obvious in every aspect of merchant shipping, from oil tankers to coasters. As the authors of *Conway's History of the Ship* put it, 'In 1900 the typical powered coaster outside the US was most probably built to a British design; by 1960 its parentage was most likely to be Dutch.'[2] This was partly due to the conservatism of the British, who clung to steam power in vessels which had changed little in the first quarter of the century.

The final handful of coastal colliers were built after the war – the last, the *James Rowan*, in 1955, – but they had the last laugh. By 1985, as Tony Lane remarked:

> By the mid-1980s almost all the traditional ship types, of which there had been such an abundance in 1975, had gone, except for the coastal trades . . . The family-controlled forty-strong Everard fleet of coasters and short-sea traders, once the butt of jokes and lordly disdain from deep-sea liner men, was one of the few dynamic shipping firms, and jobs in its fleets were sought after by men from the shrinking deep-sea fleets.'[3]

Until the 1960s ocean-going merchant ships divided into two main types, the cargo liner and the 'tramp'. In the words of the *Conway* authors,

> The tramp picked up cargo wherever it could get the best rate, and almost invariably lifted bulk goods, such as coal, coke, stone, iron ore, grain or timber. The liner had a set schedule between certain ports . . . Built for similar ports and similar conditions, tramp and liner were often alike in appearance, and often the only external difference was the cargo gear.

Cargo liners were relatively sophisticated vessels, often carrying a few dozen passengers, whose holds were subdivided into different compartments by watertight bulkheads. They were bigger and, more glamorous than the tramps, averaging between 4,000 and 8,000 tons. By 1939 they weighed in at 16 million tons, roughly double the figure for the tramps. They provided regular services to the most outlandish, as well as the most exotic, ports in the world, and their passengers were often colonial officials posted to obscure destinations in the British and French empires.

By the end of the nineteenth century, their equipment had begun to match their shape and speed for sophistication. Cargo liners with refrigerated holds were used to carry fresh meat to Britain from the Antipodes, the precursors of today's specialized carriers, while there were continuous improvements in handling equipment to reduce time in port, a factor more important than the ship's speed, since it sometimes spent only half its working life actually at sea. By the time cargo liners were doomed by the advent of container ships and jet aircraft, they were highly sophisticated vessels. The last liners ordered by Union Castle for the South African run, the *Good Hope Castle* and the *Southampton Castle*, were designed to operate alongside the company's passenger liners, and were as big (34,000 tons), and as fast – up to 25 knots – as their sisters.

The idea of the tramp steamer, the go-anywhere-carry-anything, all-purpose delivery van of the sea, dates back to before the use of steam. Tony Gloster describes a typical voyage by one of the fine Western Ocean yachts built in the little North Wales town of Porthmadog.

The *British Monarch*, an unusually attractive 4,000-ton tramp ship built on the Clyde in 1902. It was already outdated by 1912 when it was sold to the Japanese who renamed her *Luzon Maru*. She was wrecked in 1930.

A typical trip might involve taking Porthmadog slates to, for example, Papenburg in Germany about April. From there general cargos, if they were available, would be hauled to various ports of northern Europe and then on south, possibly in ballast to Cadiz, where salt would be loaded before the passage to Newfoundland. The return trip, carrying a cargo of saltfish, would be to a Mediterranean port where the master would find whatever cargo he could to enable him to be Porthmadog-bound once again, perhaps in time for Christmas.[4]

Although, as the name implies, the myth of the tramp steamer is based on the idea that it was the Wandering Jew of the world's oceans, in fact many of them had regular routes sailing from British ports. Their voyages were often based on an outward cargo of Welsh coal, and on the return journey from the Baltic or the River Plate, they usually carried grain. Indeed, in the days before radio communication, these ships were far less easy to operate in a flexible fashion than they are today.

These tramps were small, averaging 5,000 tons, and slow, averaging around 10 knots, but they made up for their small size by their numbers: in 1914 there were 2,200 of them sailing under the British flag, the core of the greatest merchant navy the world had ever seen. Improvements came fitfully. Around the turn of the century the 'whaleback' steamer used on the Great Lakes evolved into the 'turret ship', with a relatively narrow upper deck (this reduced the fees required to pass through the Suez Canal, which were based on the breadth of the upper deck). There were also many variations on the 'three island' design, in which the central upper deck was flanked by two masts complete with cranes.

The slump of the 1930s had the paradoxical outcome of effectively modernizing the British tramp fleet, because it led to the scrapping of hundreds of still seaworthy, but uneconomic, older vessels. The desire for economy had two results. The first was a steady improvement in the design of the ship itself. In the words of Frank C. Brown, tramps used to be

built as square as possible with the idea of carrying the maximum of cargo, and it was said, not untruthfully, that they had the lines of a sardine tin. All that is changed now, for the modern owner realizes that a scientifically designed hull will make all the difference to his fuel bills and surprisingly little difference to the cargo which it can carry.[5]

But he also noted the tendency for 'so much of the tramping business to fall into the hands of the cheaper flags – Greeks, Spaniards, or the peoples of the Baltic republics,' who could run the ships with cheaper crews and less rigorous safety standards. Today, of course, most merchant ships sail under more exotic flags of convenience, based in Liberia, the Bahamas and other convenient tax havens.

North Sea oil and gas keep the port of Dundee busy – the vessel in the foreground is an offshore supply ship.

As a result the British fleet numbered a mere 800 tramp ships by 1939, two-thirds fewer than in 1914, although their average age was a youthful eleven years. But the newer steam-powered ones weren't much more efficient – a 5,000-tonner still consumed 26 tons of coal a day when steaming at 11 knots, only a little less than the 30 tons required by its pre-1914 predecessor (in contrast, the equivalent diesel used under 7 tons of fuel). Even so, the wartime and postwar generation of 'general cargo' ships (by then the word tramp had become politically incorrect) were still driven by steam power – often in impressive numbers. Nearly 300 9,000- to 10,000-ton 'empire-type' ships were built on the north-east coast of England alone.

The idea of standardized ships was introduced in the First World War with mass-production at the Hog Island Shipyard in Philadelphia. But it became more routine in the Second World War, when the Americans took a British design and developed it into Liberty ships, of 7,500 gross tons, equipped with steam engines capable of 11.5 knots. By the end of the war Liberty ships – and their bigger, faster successors, the Victory ships, capable of 15 knots – were being assembled from prefabricated sections in an astonishingly short time: one Liberty ship was assembled in four days. The possibilities opened up by mass production were appreciated world-wide. One of Britain's few postwar shipbuilding success stories was the standardized 14,000-ton SD–14 type built by Austin and Pickersgill on the north-east coast.

By then the cranes used to load and unload cargo had become highly sophisticated, with four or more hatches each equipped with cranes for speed of handling. But the last tramp bought by the Reardon Smith line in 1963, the 10,000-ton *Houston City*, had been replaced within ten years by ships with their engines aft designed to carry bulk cargos. Within the decade the era of the old-fashioned general-purpose tramp, like that of the more glamorous cargo liner, had ended, almost exactly 100 years after Alfred Holt had introduced the compound engine.

The revolution which swept the shipping industry in the 1960s can be summed up in the single word 'unitization'.

This is defined by Euan Corlett as: 'the breaking down, or alternatively, the synthesis up, of goods into standardized units that can be handled by mechanized and possibly automated equipment.'[6] The traditional shipping group, owned and headquartered in Britain or other former imperial countries, was also threatened by vessels using 'flags of convenience' to avoid irksome restrictions and by the desire of dozens of emerging nations to have their own fleets, just as they all demanded their own airlines as a signal of independence.

The origins of the container ship can be traced back to the great Isambard Kingdom Brunel, who introduced cubical iron boxes to transport the local, rather crumbly, coal on his little Vale of Neath Railway in 1841. More relevant was the initiative of the United Steamship Company of Copenhagen, which in 1950 built two container-type ships for transporting Danish lager. But the container ship as we know it was the brainchild of an American, Malcolm MacLaren, who previously had nothing to do with the shipping business. In 1956 he fitted a steamship he had bought with platforms for carrying the standard trailers used in his trucking business. The idea was immediately seized on by other American ship owners, such as Matson. MacLaren hastened its spread by refusing to file patents for the key fittings required, and, for once, an international standard was quickly adopted.

Within twenty years the revolution was virtually complete, and the world's historic docks had become largely redundant – as had the hundreds of thousands of dockers and stevedores (cargo-handlers on the wharves) previously required to handle cargo. They had been replaced by thousands of containers stacked behind the docks and transported in largely standardized ships. The speed of these vessels – rising to 30 knots in some cases – and the fact that they needed to spend only a few hours in dock made it possible for express round-the-world freight services to be operated by a relatively small number of ships. The only real limitation was the dimensions of the major canals, most obviously the Panama Canal. This particular problem was

There was good overtime to be earned at the end of February 1932 by unloading foreign cargos before the imposition of a 10 per cent tariff on goods not coming from the Empire.

By 1988 many Scottish ships were reduced to importing coal for places like the power station at Leith, north of Edinburgh. The cargo was transported in ships like the 21,625-ton bulk carrier *Finnwhale*, registered, for tax purposes, in Bermuda.

solved by the adoption of what was called the 'Panamax' standard prescribing the dimensions of the largest ships that could go through the canal.

The other innovation which was to transform the world's seaways was the birth of the giant supertanker and the modern bulk carrier. The first oil tanker dates back to a ship designed by Colonel Henry Swan which was built on the Tyne in 1885. It had many of the features which still distinguish the breed: the engines were located aft; oil was carried right down to the shell of the vessel; the valves could all be operated from the main deck and the ship was designed to carry water as ballast once the oil had been delivered. While still on the stocks she was bought by a German owner

who called her *Glückauf*, after the German for 'good luck', and promptly ordered nine more.

Marcus Samuel, the founder of Shell, took the idea further, even persuading the Suez Canal Company to let his tankers through the canal (previously they had refused on grounds of safety). Samuel also arranged for special storage facilities to be installed at both ends of the long voyage to Europe from the oilfields in what were then the Dutch East Indies (now, of course, Indonesia).

In the early years of the century a system of longitudinal frames with frequent strong vertical transverse stiffeners was developed and named after a former Lloyd's surveyor, Joseph Isherwood. This created the potential for the size of

P & O's *Colombo Bay*, a classic container ship, which looks more like an advertisement for Lego than a proper ship.

tankers to be greatly increased; indeed, by 1939 the world tanker fleet weighed over 11 million tons and wartime losses were more than offset by the hundreds of standard T2 tankers built in the United States. These revealed the problems raised by the wide use of welding, which were eventually solved by using rivets at crucial seams and, above all, by the use of higher-grade steels less likely to become brittle at low temperatures.

After the war the benchmark was set by the *Velutina*, a 28,000-tonner built by Swan Hunter on the Tyne and delivered to Shell in 1950. Then came two key events: the shift in the location of oil refineries, formerly sited near the oilfields, to areas nearer the consumers, and the closure of the Suez Canal in 1956. While refineries remained distant from their markets, relatively small tankers were required to transport individual products, from fuel oil and petrol to specialized chemicals. According to Euan Corlett: 'Shell alone loaded at twenty-five ports and discharged at ten times as many.' Once the refineries had been moved nearer to the markets tankers needed to be as big as possible to carry crude oil from the oilfields, generally in the Persian Gulf, to Europe, and, increasingly, to Japan as well.

By forcing tankers to take the far longer route round the Cape of Good Hope, the closure of the Suez Canal encouraged owners to build tankers far larger than the 35,000-tonners which had used the canal. In fact 'far larger' is a gross understatement: the *Universe Apollo*, the first 100,000-ton tanker, or VLCC (Very Large Crude Carrier), was built in 1959, by which time tankers of above the Suez limit accounted for an eighth of the world's tonnage. In under twenty years the *Universe Apollo* had been dwarfed by ULCCs (Ultra Large Crude Carriers), monsters five times its size, and tankers of 300,000 tons were commonplace. Then came a hangover in the wake of the slump in the world's thirst for oil, caused by the oil crises of 1973–74 and 1979, and since then sizes have not increased further, largely because the million-tonners discussed so confidently in the early 1970s would have been impractical to handle. There were, in the end, limits to the advantages of scale.

The big advances in the past twenty years have been in increasing the safety of vessels which, if they leaked, could (and did) cause havoc, as witnessed by the crisis sparked by the *Torrey Canyon*, which spilt its oil over the Scilly Isles in 1967, and the *Exxon Valdez*, which did the same thing in Alaska nearly a quarter of a century later. Impressive-sounding systems like COW (Crude Oil Washing), SBT (Segregated Ballast Tanks) and IGS (Inert Gas Systems) have done much to reduce the hazards.

The bulk carrier dates back even further than the oil tanker, to the first coastal collier, the *John Bowes*, which was built as long ago as 1852. Then came the ships designed to carry metallic ore on the Great Lakes, and smaller vessels dedicated to all sorts of purposes, including the *Bacchus*, a ship specially adapted in 1935 to carry wine from Algeria across the Mediterranean to France. More mundane cargos included bulk chemicals. Again, it was the 1960s and 1970s which saw the bulk carrier develop into the third most dominant type of ship to sail the world's oceans. Nevertheless, many of them were not devoted to a single type of cargo.

There were a great many ships designed to carry oil, metallic ores or bulk commodities of other descriptions, hence the sobriquet OBO (Oil Bulk Ore). Their flexibility ensured that they did not suffer from the problem faced by oil tankers, namely that they carried cargos in only one direction.

Yet the general drive towards increasing specialization ensured that tankers were more typical of modern merchant fleets than the OBOs and modern world-scale industry has produced requirements for dozens of even more specialized vessels. Technically, the most extraordinary are the tankers used to carry liquefied gases, which need to be kept at mind-bogglingly low temperatures – below -160°C in some cases – over thousands of miles. Gases must be transported in liquid form to reduce their otherwise unmanageable bulk – liquid methane occupies 630 times less space than the gas. The first specialized gas carriers, such as the aptly named *Methane Pioneer*, were developed at the end of the 1950s to bring gas to Britain from the Algerian fields. But the discovery of North Sea gas, together with the industrial rise of fuel-hungry Japan, meant that the most spectacular new ships were required to carry gas from south-east Asia to Japan.

Less exotic novelties included ships adapted to carry thousands of cars, mostly from Japan to the west coast of the United States. These, perhaps more than any other vessel, distilled the essence of the new revolution, for they were more like floating car parks than the tramp ships of yore. As Corlett said: 'Ships have become links in transport systems rather than the system itself,' and, as mere links, are perhaps best studied in an industrial rather than a shipping context.

The handful of people who operate the modern container ship or tanker, spending most of their time on watch looking at computer screens, are also a far cry from the seamen of old. And despite the disappearance of the perceived romance traditionally associated with a sailor's life, it's a lot less squalid nowadays. The contrast between the imaginary romance and the grim reality was superbly caught by the currently underrated English poet John

Masefield. One of his most famous poems, 'Cargoes', sets the contrast out starkly enough, between the

Quinquireme of Ninevah from distant Ophir
Rowing home to haven in sunny Palestine,
With a cargo of ivory,
And apes and peacocks,
Sandalwood, cedarwood, and sweet white wine

and the

Dirty British coaster with a salt-caked smoke stack,
Butting through the Channel in the mad March days,
With a cargo of Tyne coal,
Road-rail, pig-lead,
Firewood, iron-ware, and cheap tin trays.

The appeal is most clearly expressed in 'Sea Fever', which became famous after it had been set to music by John Ireland. 'I must go down to the seas again, to the lonely sea and the sky,' for 'the call of the running tide/Is a wild call and a clear call that may not be denied.'

Only too often seamen signed on for less than romantic reasons – indeed, in 'Hell's Kitchen', Masefield shows himself fully aware of the harshness of the life of the sailor who swears that when he's discharged and draws his pay 'I won't come to sea no more.' But the money, of course, didn't last, 'For he painted the atmosphere blue,' and

He shipped a week later with the clothes upon his back,
He had to pinch a little straw, he had to beg a sack
To sleep on, when his watch was through – so he did.

Perhaps the grimmest of all is the poem 'Bill' about the death of a seafarer:

He lay dead on the cluttered deck and stared at the cold skies,
With never a friend to mourn for him nor a hand to close
   his eyes:
'Bill, he's dead,' was all they said; 'he's dead, 'n' there he lies...
'It's rough about Bill,' the fo'c's'le said, 'we'll have to stand
   his wheel.

Not surprisingly, thousands of seamen deserted every year. Captain A.G. Course records how 'the consul at Pernambuco reported that hardly a ship arrived there without the seamen complaining of brutality, starvation, insulting language and of their ship being shorthanded. In nine cases out of ten he was obliged to find in favour of the men.'[7] Unfortunately, if the seamen refused duty because the ships were overloaded, they could be, and regularly were, imprisoned – over 2,000 of them in the three years from 1870 to 1873 alone.

In principle at least, life became less bestial after the reforms of the late 1880s. These included the introduction of the 'Plimsoll Line'* designed to prevent overloading and legislation passed by Joseph Chamberlain abolishing the evil system of 'advance notes', which could be cashed only ten days after the ship sailed – and at a hefty discount, and to the advantage of the middle-men who recruited the hapless sailors, especially the owners of their lodgings, evil men called 'boarding masters' or 'crimps'.

Even then, British ship owners found ways round the regulations, continuing to overload by what George Young, the veteran maritime correspondent of the *Cape Times*, described as 'hogging' their ships:

The ends were pressed down by weight of cargo, while
the centre on which the loadline was painted was
pressed up. Other ship owners even saw fit to paint out
the official marks and replace them with others set
higher up the side of the ship. Then again, there were
owners who sailed their ships after dark so that the
loadline could not be observed.[8]

Both the mythical appeal of sailing, and the appalling reality lasted until astonishingly recently. George Young describes conditions before the Second World War.

Lights were turned off at night to save coal, and oil
lamps were used . . . [other European nations insisted
that their crews at least had the benefit of electric light]
. . . The steamers covered only 230 miles [370km] a day,
voyages were excruciatingly long, and the bill of fare was

Overleaf: The apparent glamour of the bulk oil business: the 44,700-ton *Colorado* unloading at the Hound Point oil terminal on the Firth of Forth.

monotonous . . . Fresh food was consumed in the first fortnight of the voyage and after that the fare was canned meat and vegetables, corned beef, and dried tack . . . if the food was often in short supply, so was the drinking water, because the boilers had to be filled first.

Tony Lane records how a veteran who went to sea early in the Second World War also found that 'there was no bathroom. You bathed out on deck out of a bucket. The hot water you got was from dripping joints or valves on steam pipes from the engine.' Yet still the glamour persisted. As Lane comments, 'To live on ships and the sea is to be *different*, and seafarers are very conscious and vocal about being a "race apart", though it is never exactly clear what they mean by it.' He quotes a youngster who signed on as a steward's boy in the late 1960s. He had grown up in the south end of Liverpool's dockland. 'Living next door was a bosun. He had this big map of all the places he used to go...and then, coming from a big family with seven brothers and sisters, it seemed like an ideal way to get away from home.' However, it was usually sheer necessity that attracted recruits even at times of theoretically full employment. 'I had no great desire to be a seaman', said another youngster. 'I went to get a job. It was either that or go digging, because I didn't have any qualifications for anything else.'

The strain also told on the captains. Young recalls one drunk who issued the command: 'If ever you see a red light on either bow give two blasts once a fortnight.' In another bizarre incident a young officer poured a kettleful of scalding hot tea down the voicepipe to his drunken captain, threw the kettle overboard and assured him that he was having hallucinations when he mounted to the bridge. 'And the captain stopped drinking for at least a week,' remarks Young.

Many of the owners came up through the ranks of the more sober captains. One such was Sir Anthony Gloster, whose strength and ruthlessness were superbly caught by Rudyard Kipling in his long poem 'The Mary Gloster'. The dying ship owner tells his spoiled, gently bred son how he

> Took the chances they wouldn't, an' now they're calling
> it luck.
> Lord, what boats I've handled – rotten and leaky and old –
> Ran 'em – opened the bilge-cock, precisely as I was told.
> Grub that 'ud bind you crazy, and crews that 'ud turn you
> grey,
> And a big fat lump of insurance to cover the risk on the
> way.

As for the ones who didn't believe, why, 'They've served me since as skippers.' And how did he and his wife start?

> When we bought half-shares in a cheap 'un and
> hoisted a flag of our own.
> Patching and coaling on credit, and living the Lord
> knew how.
> We started the Red Ox freighters – we've eight and
> thirty now.

It wasn't just timing, it was foresight, too.

> I knew – I knew what was coming, when we bid on the
> *Byfleet's* keel
> They piddled and piffled with iron. I'd given more
> orders for steel!

However bad conditions were in peacetime, the merchant navy suffered worse in wartime. As we saw in Chapter 1, and as C.B.A. Behrens points out in her history of the Second World War. 'It seems not unlikely that a quarter of the men who were in the merchant navy at the outbreak of war, and perhaps an even higher proportion, did not survive until the end . . . Nothing of this sort, it seems, can have been experienced in any fighting service considered as a whole.'[9] Many ship owners made matters worse by stopping the pay of seamen whose ships had been sunk, on the grounds that they were by definition unemployed from then on.

Of course, the sea had always had the capacity to be more threatening even than the U-boats. This passage in Nicholas Monsarrat's *The Cruel Sea*, which describes a convoy on its way to the northern Russian port of Murmansk, could have been written about any winter storm on any of the world's oceans.

Huge waves, a mile from crest to crest, roared down upon the pigmies that were to be their prey; sometimes the entire surface of the water would be blown bodily away, and any ship that stood in the path of the onslaught shook and staggered as tons of green sea smote her upper deck and raced in a torrent down her whole length . . . Even when the green seas withheld their blows for a moment, the wind, screaming and clawing at the rigging, struck fear into every heart; for if deck-gear and canvas screens could vanish, perhaps even men could be whipped away by its furious strength.

And in the words of the greatest of seagoing writers, Joseph Conrad, 'The ocean has the conscienceless temper of a savage autocrat spoiled by too much adulation . . . The most amazing wonder of the deep is its unfathomable cruelty.'

The Cruel Sea, that now under-appreciated epic of wartime convoys, starred Jack Hawkins with his naturally jutting jaw.

* Named after Samuel Plimsoll, the MP who pushed through the legislation required. In fact the initiative came from a Tyneside ship owner, James Hall. Plimsoll took up the cause, perhaps because he felt guilty about the fact that he had made his fortune from coal being carried to London by rail, traffic which hit coasters and their seamen.

BOATS AT WORK

THE WORKHORSES, the delivery vans of Britain's waterways, came in all shapes and sizes – tugs and barges, lighters and coasters, and many other types. Up to and during the railway era they transported Britain's food, its coal, its bricks and its grain. They ventured away from the country's shores and fussed round bigger ships, towing them in and out of port, into and out of their berths, helping them to load and unload. They were the workboats, thousands of them.

Of all types of ship these have the most romantic names, each encapsulating some feature required for the river or estuary in which it sailed, the special cargo it carried. Some of the more esoterically named examples are listed in the feature on page 86. The Tyne had its own keel, its own wherry, the Rye and Arun their own barges. These were, originally, boats designed to be sailed, rowed or punted up and down Britain's tidal rivers and, sometimes, daringly, out to sea. Indeed, coastal craft date back so far that C.R. Benstead[1] traced them back to two ancient influences, Viking and Breton. The Viking, which had a clinker-built double-ended hull pointed at both stem and stern, was used on the east coast and into the Channel as far as Dorset, while the Breton-type boat, which had a smooth, carvel-built hull and a transom or square stern, was naturally

found round the west coast. The designs were adapted to the different conditions, one to the shelving sands of the North Sea coastline, the other to the rocky Atlantic shore.

One of the great survivors of the oldest traditions was the Severn trow (pronounced to rhyme with 'go'). This boat is first mentioned in an official document dated 1411, but clearly it was already well established by then, and had probably been in use since the time of the Vikings five centuries earlier. Like so many of their kind, the trows relied on man (or horse) power if wind and tide did not suffice. In adverse conditions the journey downstream from Shrewsbury to Gloucester could take up to a month, but if there was a 'fresh' – floodwater racing down from the Welsh mountains – it could be accomplished in a couple of days. Like many similar craft, trows were immensely long lived – the *William*, built in Shrewsbury in 1809, traded until 1939 before being wrecked. Trows, like other workboats, lasted even longer. Of all workboats, perhaps the most romantic was the Galway Hooker, which 'sat on the water like a seagull' and carried turf round the Irish coasts until well into the 1970s.

The variety was endless: some workboats, like the Clyde gravel smacks, were more like coasters than simple river craft, as were the West Country's outside barges and the Mersey's jigger flats. The heyday of sailing ships in the

Typical maritime traffic jam on the Thames in the shadow of Tower Bridge.

south-east lasted into the second half of the nineteenth century; and on the Severn in particular, with its 4-knot tides and brisk breezes, sail power remained competitive until very recently – Eric McKee[2] cites the *John*, built of iron in 1840 and still afloat in 1939.

As we shall see in Chapter 6, workboats were also adapted for leisure. The dictionary definition of punt, for instance, is 'a flat-bottomed shallow boat, broad and square both ends, propelled by a pole thrust against the bottom of the river', and it is generally pictured as being full of white-flannelled undergraduates. But some types, especially on the south coast, were deep-water 'hovellers', used as ferries across rivers or to ships at anchor.

Workboats were first classed by their usage, then, in the days of sail, by the type of rigging – the number of masts was less important. Some, like the Severn punt, were found only in one river or, like the Scottish coble, scattered along a whole coastline; others, such as the stem keel boat with a transom, were seemingly omnipresent. But as time went on only a few of the fittest types survived, although examples of many others have been lovingly restored, often by individual enthusiasts. Most of these boats survived the railway era, partly because carriage by water was cheaper, partly because the railway companies sometimes preferred to share the traffic with coasters. But they disappeared between the wars with the rise of the motor lorry.

A tug bustles past the historic Tynemouth Priory on the Tyne estuary.

ORIGINALLY THE WORD 'WHERRY' meant any small, fast-oared boat used for carrying people and goods. Some time in the late eighteenth century, writes Peter Smith,

The shipwrights adapted the double-ended hull of the small passenger-carrying wherry and stepped the mast up in the eyes of the ship and rigged her with a large fore-and-aft mainsail, its high peak designed to catch the lightest breeze on the Broads' tree-fringed waters . . . it was also the last sailing boat to carry a 'bonnet' perched on top of the mast.

The traditional Norfolk trading wherry, with its large, unencumbered 35ft (10.7m) hold, combined the superior handling qualities of the passenger wherry with the carrying capacity of its predecessor, the Norfolk keel, based on the Viking longboat which it soon replaced. With its fore-and-aft sails the wherry could sail almost directly into the wind, a feature which at first led the people of the Broads to believe that the boats were connected with black magic.

In the early years of the nineteenth century the three main Norfolk rivers were developed and canals dug between them to produce the system of Broadland waterways whose remains are still so heavily used by pleasure craft today. The heyday of the wherry was between 1850 and 1900, when it carried 'corn and coal' (the latter sometimes from ships moored well off-shore, proof of their hardiness) as well as timber, logs, bricks, fertilizer and any other heavy cargo required by the rich farms of Norfolk.

Like so many other river vessels, they declined with the arrival of the motor lorry – indeed, there were only thirty left by 1930. But by then they had evolved into pleasure vessels. Two anonymous adventurers started off the trend by taking a wherry into the then-deserted heart of the Broads with a gun and a fishing rod and living for a year off what they managed to catch and shoot.

At first the wherries were converted into houseboats just for the summer season, reverting to their usual role during the winter.

But soon bastard wherries appeared, with the stern lengthened to give room for passengers to relax. This 'wherry yacht', says Smith, 'was not a true wherry at all, but a wherry-rigged barge yacht, carvel-built'. Unfortunately, of all the thousands of pleasureboats which still throng the Broads, only three wherry yachts remain, including the last one ever built, the *White Moth*. It was properly constructed of mahogany and pine as late as 1915 and still gives the feel, at once relaxed and workmanlike, of its breed.

The *White Moth,* one of the few remaining Norfolk wherries.

Thames barges on the lower reaches of the river in 1977: an impressive sight even though they were no longer working for their living.

Workboats were generally centred at what McKee calls 'bridge towns', the first point in an estuary which was bridged, sometimes well upstream – an extreme case, York, is 53 miles (85km) from the sea. Their trades could be immensely complicated. Michael Bouquet describes one particular traffic.

Beach boats were run on to the Sussex beaches to collect rounded flint pebbles known locally as 'boulders'. The open yawl-rigged boats which did this work were known as 'boulder boats'. They brought their cargos into Newhaven, where the stones were landed until a sufficient quantity had been accumulated to load a coaster or a brig. Ships like these would take the stones to Runcorn, where they would be offloaded again into narrow boats which took them to the Potteries.[3]

It was the Thames that brought together every possible type of working vessel, together with the many trades required to man and service them. As late as 1938 Frank C. Brown[4] compiled a long list of operating boats. Some, like the banana-carriers, were high-sea ships, but most were confined to the Thames and its estuary. The public services used many different types: the customs launch, the health authority launch, the harbour service launch. The Port of London

Authority had its own dredgers, the London County Council its own sludge vessel and the fire brigade its fire floats. Most of the others – including ships like the *Flatiron*, which had to be specially designed to fit under the numerous low bridges on the way to Wandsworth Gas Works – were privately owned and designed for specific cargos.

Probably the most famous of them all were the Thames sailing barges. They were not designed for a particular purpose; rather they evolved over the centuries through trial and error into unique flat-bottomed carriers able to cope with shallow rivers, yet also capable of crossing the North Sea – they had detachable lee boards so that they could sit on the mud at low tide. As Peter Smith explains,

> Crewed only by a skipper and a mate, their cargo consisted of anything and everything to anywhere from any place. Hay from the East Anglian farms to feed the thousands of London horses in the nineteenth century, bricks to build the sprawling metropolis . . .and the transshipment of other cargo from the Pool of London and the docks downriver to the customer.[5]

By the end of the nineteenth century there were around 2,000 of these sailing barges, but they became early victims of the lorry. The last, named, appropriately, the *Cabby* – the boat and its predecessors were London's jobbing carriers, albeit of goods rather than people – was built in 1928. By 1939 there were only 600 Thames barges left. Today the only survivor in its original shape is the *Cambria*, built just after the First World War, a boat which fulfilled its role until 1971, when it was saved by the Maritime Trust.

Almost as ubiquitous were the Thames tugs. The Thames was not the first river to use tugs: the Clyde and the Tyne can both claim precedence, and other rivers and harbours also bred their own, although they all corresponded to the rules described by M.K. Stammers. 'The hull design of a harbour tug is based on a series of compromises. It has to be as short as possible for dock working but capable of going to sea. It needs a deep draught for stability and to keep the propeller well immersed for maximum power, but not so deep that it cannot surmount the sill of the dock gates.'[6]

The Thames tug trade was made by the Crimean War, during which the huge number of ships carrying men and munitions to the front required an equally unprecedented number of tugs. When peace came in 1856 they sought work – 'seeking' was the phrase – towing sailing ships to and from the Thames as far as the Downs, the great marshalling yard of sailing ships off the Thanet coast. Lacking work there, they ventured further afield looking for ships to salvage. The Downs also bred another type of trade, 'hovelling' – the transport of the many goods required by these ships, from mail and food to general ship's chandlery, a service often performed by the Deal luggers. Even more specialized were the pilot cutters, designed to shelter pilots who sometimes, in the days of sail and before radio, had to wait for days for their clients in the choppiest of seas. With their beautiful lines and excellent handling, Bristol pilot cutters are a particular favourite of amateur enthusiasts.

A beauty restored. The lovingly polished boiler and single-cylinder engine of a launch aptly named the *Fire Queen*.

Tugs like this could be called fussy, but despite their 'one candle-power engines', and even with their funnels lowered to sail under a low bridge, they could still cope with a whole train of barges.

Just as sailing barges continued for longer than would seem economically likely, so did tugs with paddles rather than screw propellers, for twin paddles, each separately powered, made them extremely manoeuvrable and helped them to survive until the 1960s – even though screw propulsion, combined with high-pressure boilers, had become widespread ninety years earlier. But they remained chronically underpowered. One veteran, Bill Lindley, remembered: 'They were small little tugs that had to rely on tides as well. They were all steam tugs and they only had about two candle horsepower.'[7]

The arrival of larger, steam-driven ships merely changed the type of work: the larger the liner, the more help it needed to handle its entry and departure from its berth. And until the end of the century there were still a good number of sailing freighters requiring longer hauls. Despite their lack of power these steam tugs managed to tow far larger vessels – and they were built to last. Typical was the clinker-built, steam-driven *Uncle Sam*, built in Blackwall in 1849, which was the first merchant ship to pass under Tower Bridge (it slipped through in the wake of the launch which officially declared the bridge open). After half a century's service, most profitably helping to tow clipper ships the last few miles to their berth and thus saving up to a week's sailing time, she was sold to be broken up in Holland.

The staple work for *Uncle Sam* and its successors was towing the Thames barges which at one time numbered nearly 10,000. For much of the nineteenth century the barges were unpowered, simply drifting up and down river on the tide offloading from ocean-going ships which often preferred not to tie up at wharves, so tempting for light-fingered locals. There were many varieties of sailing lighters. During the nineteenth century they were steadily replaced by what were called the 'dumb lighter' – dumb because it was unpowered, 'lighter' because one of its original uses was to lighten a ship's load so that it could reach the shallower, upper reaches of the river. The dumb lighter, simply a cut-down seagoing vessel, also came in many shapes and sizes, but the Thames produced its own type, specially designed to be easily towed at any stage of the tide.

Tidal power was slow, and, in any case, the replacement of the old open wharves with docks meant that the lighters had to be pushed and pulled into position. This required a special type of tug, the craft tug, to which the adjective 'fussy' is usually applied. Frank Brown well understood their peculiarities:

> They all give the impression of being pushed up forward, the reason for this being the desire to have the towing hook as neatly amidships as possible, and in order to give the necessary buoyancy for the heavy weights in the bows their lines forward are very full, so that when they are running free at full speed they raise a big bow-wave and assume an air of tremendous importance . . . although the forward lines are bluff . . . the after lines of their run are usually as sweet as those of a yacht.

In spite of their self-important demeanour and bow-wave, 'There is no doubt that they do their work remarkably efficiently,' he asserts. Like the Thames barges, these tugs resembled the London taxi – both squat, both ridiculous at first sight, both admirably adapted to the conditions peculiar to the Thames and London's narrow streets. The craft tug generally had single screws (twin screws might have fouled ropes) and they remained coal-powered and steam-driven, not only because the operators were conservative, but also because the more modern diesel–electric tugs cost so much more to build, notwithstanding a considerable saving in running costs because diesels used so much less fuel when merely ticking over.

All these workhorses were needed to supply what was, until 1939, a river bordered not just by docks, but also by innumerable factories up and downstream of the docks. As a result the working-class community living on the banks of the Thames was not confined to dockers, bargees and warehousemen; it also included thousands of industrial workers. As one veteran, Nell Combes, told a group of historians, for *On the River, Memories of a Working River*, 'Everybody was attached to the

Unloading Danish bacon in a hurry at Hays Wharf just before the deadline of February 29th 1932 and the introduction of the 10 per cent Empire preference tariff.

Traditional freight: unloading frozen meat, probably lamb from New Zealand, at London's Victoria Docks.

river in some way or other, whether they were dockers, warehousemen, or ordinary labourers moving all the grain from the warehouses and loading. Everything was to do with the riverside.' Indeed, the docklands were a famously close-knit community. Their inhabitants trusted each other, left doors open; the kids were able to get bread and dripping from any of their friends' mums. But it was not a romantic world, life and work were hard and labour more often casual than not, even if the lightermen, the aristocrats of the river, were assured of a lifetime of well-paid employment.

There were factories of every description. Probably the most important processed 'industrial' as opposed to 'natural' food, though even 'natural' products such as tea needed to be sorted into packets, inevitably in factories near the docks where it had been unloaded. Nell Combes remembered:

'There were girls who worked alongside the river, most of them in the tinned fruit and the currants and the soft fruit warehouses. Other girls worked in the CWS (Cooperative Wholesale Society) doing bags of rice.' Wally Shreve recalled the factories along the north bank.

There was Foster's, the beer bottler, then W.C. Henley's, the cable works, then the Western Electric that became the Standard. Next door to there was Griffith's Wharf with the Glassblower's, then came Loaders and Ukeline, the margarine manufacturers; then comes the largest factory of the lot, Tate & Lyle's Silvertown [Docklands' only surviving major factory], then the India Rubber Company, known as Silver's, who made the material that they insulate cables with, and tennis balls, golf balls, India rubbers, all sorts. Then came Keiller's, the jam and sweet people, then came the CWS. The opposite side of the road was the flour mills, Joseph Rank's, Mellish's, all just inside the big dock, they all came off the piers. There was Brunner Mond and, further down, Knight's, the soap factory.

Like many of the other factories, Knight's was instantly recognizable by its smell, a recurrent theme with many river veterans like Tom Sawyer.

You'd be amazed the amount of smells you could get walking up the road here in Bermondsey. There was the finest soap factory, I think, in Great Britain, called Atkinson's. You'd have the leather trade here, and the glue factory next to it. You'd have the beautiful scent from the soap factory, and right next door you'd have the glue factory where you'd boil up bones and that.

Another old timer, Alan Godfrey, pointed out: 'All the obnoxious industries, like John Knight's soap works, bought parcels of land on the Thames to get free waterage.'

Transport problems in London Docks in October 1920 led to enormous piles of sugar building up on the quayside, a scene foreshadowing wartime London with its omnipresent piles of sandbags.

FROM BALDIE TO ZULU

In his book on working boats, Eric McKee provides a selection of some of the more outlandish names he came across. These included:

Baldie A south-eastern Scottish variety of fife, which emerged about 1860 when Garibaldi was unifying Italy.

Bog The small 25ft (7.6m) class of Hastings lugger weighing 4 to 7 tons. The word may have come from 'bogue', meaning to fall off the wind.

Boggy A double-ended lugger from the west coast of Scotland.

Calf, cauf A 12-to-16ft (3.7–4.9m) tender to a large coble, mule or yawl. Usually found in the form of a coble.

Coble One of the family of east-coast boats which have square sterns, plank keels and divide into English and Scottish types.

Doble A 12-to-18ft (3.7–5.5m) Medway fishing boat. A double-ender.

Farm An early five-man boat from Yorkshire.

Folyer, Volyer A boat up to 20ft (6.1m) in length which shot the net to close the main Cornish pilchard seine. Dialect variation of 'follower'.

Flash boat An extreme four-oared West Country racing shell.

Funny An extreme design of 20-to-30ft (6.1–9.2m) Thames racing skiff.

Gabbart A double-ended sailing lighter of the Clyde estuary, about 40ft (12.2m) long and able to pass through the Forth–Clyde canal.

Lerret A four- or six-oared mackerel seine boat used off Chesil Bank. The name is said to come from *Lady of Loretto*, the prototype.

Mule, Mulie The under 4-ton class of Brixham trawler, the double-ended coble or the Thames barge with a standing gaff mizen. Some cross-breeding is implied in all cases.

Mumble-bee A 35-to-40ft (10.7–12.2m), 17-ton Brixham trawler, single-masted with a few ketch conversions. The name is said to have once been bumble-bee, but it changed when they began to land catches at Mumbles, near Swansea.

Nabby 32-to-34ft (9.75–10.4m) open great line luggers of the Clyde estuary, which replaced the earlier smacks.

Nobby A large family of 20-to-35ft (6.1–10.7m) shoal keel boats, largely decked and cutter-rigged, found between Tremadoc Bay and the Solway Firth and used for many purposes.

Picarooner A 15ft (4.6m) fishing lugger from Clovelly. Once the name of a type of pirate's boat, though the term is far from relevant any longer.

Pram (or Praam) A square-ended tender with plank keel.

Shoe A 20ft (6.1m) box-shaped train barge on the Taunton–Bridgwater canal.

Shout An old, double-ended, flat-bottom barge of the Thames and Severn. The name comes from Dutch scuit.

Shinerman A 22-to-24ft (6.7–7.3m) part-decked mackerel beach lugger from Eastbourne.

Tosher A one- or two-masted lugger, just under 20ft (6.1m) long at Mevagissey, but a 40ft (12.2m) gaff-rigged smack in Ramsgate. 'Toshing' was taking copper from laid-up warships, a shady term that was apt for a class made just short enough to miss harbour dues.

Zulu A 55-to-80ft (16.8–24.4m) Scottish drifter with a fifie's plumb stem and a scaffie's raked stern. She had a dipping lug fore and a standing lug mizen and was built at the time of the Zulu War of 1879.

A still-busy river. Workboats bustling around at Renfrew on the Clyde.

Until the middle of the nineteenth century the Thames had been a great shipbuilding centre, with all the attendant coopers' yards, ropewalks and workshops making such essentials as block and tackle. Its high point came when Brunel launched his giant and ill-fated *Great Eastern*, but the arrival of ironclads like this sentenced London's shipbuilding to a lingering death. It finally expired just before the First World War. But the era of iron and steel led to the establishment of engineering works on the South Bank, whose relics included the shot tower that formed such a feature of the Festival of Britain in 1951.

London might have required an ever-increasing supply of bricks and mortar (even in modern times most of the materials needed to build Canary Wharf were brought in giant barges), but coal was always the mainstay of river traffic. Colliers bearing coal, principally from the Tyne, for the gasworks and tar distilleries were a familiar part of the Thames scene for several centuries. Modern methods of power generation merely increased the demand for river-borne coal and then oil. The Gas Light and Coke Company had opened the giant Beckton* Gasworks in the 1850s. It was served by, among many other boats, the *Britannia*, the oldest surviving tug, which was built in 1893 and fitted with diesel engines to replace its steam engines as late as 1955. With electricity came power stations. The first high-voltage power station in the world was built by Ferranti at Deptford in 1889, to be followed by the well-known landmarks at Battersea, Bankside and Lots Road, all fed by 'sea coal' (or 'sea oil'). Until it closed, well after the Second World War, the demand for coal to feed the Beckton works was met by special colliers owned by the Gas Light and Coke Company.

These featured a funnel decorated with two dark rings and red spikes designed to imitate a gas ring (one, built as late as 1936, was even called 'Mr Therm' in honour of a major advertising campaign of the time).

The Thames was also the home of coasters which ventured further from the British coast, across the North Sea, the Channel, and even the Bay of Biscay to Bordeaux, 'from whence', wrote Frank Brown, 'come fruit, wine, nuts, resin, turpentine and many other commodities . . . The Hamburg ships bring sugar from the centre of Europe, fruit, toys, glassware etc. The Dutch services carry large quantities of foodstuffs, especially pork and mutton, cheese, sugar, butter, margarine, bulbs . . . live eels by the thousand make quite an interesting sideline.' Not all of these ships were British. During the First World War the Dutch made considerable profits by building sailing coasters with auxiliary engines while new motor ships, with shallower draughts allowing them to get closer to the tidal wharves, were used in the trade to the northern coast of France.

Perhaps the oddest and most original of all the ships were the 'rabbit boats' used to import thousands of rabbits caught on the sand dunes of the coast of Belgium. These had rounded cruiser sterns to help them manoeuvre in and out of their berths in Ostend, a fashion later copied by other merchant ships, not to aid handling but because they allowed greater speed. But even before the 1939–1945 war the shape of things to come was seen in the refrigerated ships operating between the Thames and the Baltic. The cargo was all in parcels, and the hulls subdivided, the first sign of the container revolution that was to sweep away the old world so completely after the war.

Trinity Docks in 1866 when shipbuilding on the Thames was declining because of the ever-increasing size of ships and the use of iron and steel.

*Named after Mr Beck, the governor of the company.

THE FISHERMEN OF ENGLAND – AND SCOTLAND

ONCE UPON A TIME, until 1914 at least, fishing was a major industry in Britain, employing over 100,000 people. It is only in the past twenty years, above all since our ill-starred entry into the so-called European Union, that it has fallen into an apparently irreversible decline. For historical reasons, then, fishing boats, writes Eric McKee, 'form the largest group of working boat types' although, as he admits, 'just about any sort of boat can be used for fishing one way or another'.[1] The variety is enormous even if lack of space prevents any description of the deep-sea fishermen sallying forth beyond the continental shelf to the Arctic Sea and Newfoundland.

Fishermen themselves have confused the situation by muddling categories. C.R. Benstead remarks: 'When in the same breath, he talks about a trawler, a ketch and a dandy from Brixham, he is not, as you might think, referring to three different craft; he is merely talking about one of the old Brixham fishing smacks.'[2] To the sailor, writes Benstead, 'anything that is lug-rigged is naturally a lugger . . . anything from a Yarmouth yawl to a Manx nickie, a Sennen crabber, or even, astonishingly, a Scottish zulu'.

Nevertheless, these many and various boats did have some features in common: above all, that sail lingered on for decades in the form of the Scottish zulus and the Cornish luggers and even until today in the oyster dredgers of Falmouth. Their sails are protected by an old law that prohibits the use of engines in the fishery, a regulation which has helped to preserve both the fishery itself and the classic sailing fleet which dredges at the mouth of the Helford River. Drifting silently with the tide in one of these beautiful wooden boats, it is said that it is so quiet that you can talk to someone several hundred yards away. Alas, other types, like the Morecambe Bay prawners, probably the fastest fishing boats ever built, are now extinct.

The most common type of fishing boat is the lugger, also called a driver or a drifter, which has two masts, a foremast and a mizen mast and is worked by eight men. It was developed in Scotland and Cornwall – in fact, half the luggers on the west coast of Scotland had originally come from Cornwall, but once they'd travelled north they were renamed boggies (and in faraway Hastings on the Sussex coast they were known as Bogs), a term supposedly derived from 'bogue', meaning to fall off the wind, as these luggers tended to do.

The basic Cornish lugger with its two (or even three) masts, each with a square sail and a topsail on a tack, was perfected by the French with their *chasse-marées*, which were used as privateers during the Napoleonic Wars and copied by the Cornish fishermen. Keith Harris explains:

Fishing boats at Looe flying the Canadian flag in April 1995 to show their support for the Canadians who had just sent intrusive Spanish fishermen packing.

Fishing for flounder under the old Waterloo Bridge in the days before the Thames became truly polluted.

Whatever their detailed design, they were all tough and immensely seaworthy. In 1854 a 45ft (13.7m) fishing lugger, the *Mystery*, sailed from Cornwall to Melbourne in a mere four months and in the 1980s the Brickhill family – including four children – sailed their eighty-four-year-old Looe lugger *Guide Me* to South Africa and Brazil. Judy Brickhill says:

Looe luggers have very low freeboards; they sit on their bilge which gives them very good balance. She stands up well because she's a fishing boat, built to go fast and built to carry loads of fish and to function in any kind of weather. It's not the boat that cracks, it's the people . . . She's hard work to sail – often with a lugger you have to take the whole sail down and put it up on the other side of the mast – but she can go at fantastic speeds.[4]

To the layman one lugger was much like another, usually a tarred black hull with her home-port numbers and a couple of strakes picked out in white, topped off with a suit of sails which were any shade of tan through to near black . . . however, a fisherman could tell at a glance where a boat hailed from . . . thus the luggers from Looe, Polperro, Fowey and Mevagissey were built with square transoms, whilst the St Ives, Penzance and Newlyn boats were invariably double-enders, i.e. pointed at both bow and stern...smaller boats known locally as 'gaffers' came mostly from Polperro . . . at Mevagissey they were called 'toshers' and an increase in harbour fees for boats over the length of 20ft (6.1m) resulted in the canny local fishermen ordering boats measuring 19ft 11in.[3]

Basically there seem to have been two different types, the bigger mackerel luggers, up to 52ft (15.8m) in length, and the smaller pilchard luggers of about 32ft (9.75m). Both were generally built on the beach itself. But the variations on each type were seemingly endless. The Mount's Bay lugger, for instance, was developed with a pointed stem so that more of them could be packed into the smaller harbours west of the Lizard.

The smack, the other type of vessel most commonly used for fishing, has varied even more widely. As Mike Smylie writes, they 'had developed all over the British Isles so that no particular type was typical of any one area. There were transom-sterned smacks, counter-sterned smacks and, to a lesser degree, round-sterned smacks. They had evolved from the Norske influence, similar to the larger gabbarts.'[5] Another type, gigs with a crew of four (three oarsmen and a cox), were used as fast, easily launched beach boats handling for mackerel and hake. They are now preserved purely as pleasureboats, even though sailing them in anything but the lightest of breezes remains extremely tricky.

The muddy, sandy, quirky east coast of Britain produced some of the most extraordinary kinds of boat. There was the Thames bawley, with its open coal fire in the middle for cooking the shrimps. 'At first,' writes C.R. Benstead, 'a bawley was just a boat that caught and boiled shrimps in the boiler she carried, but time extended the term to cover the type of craft, whatever her catch.' With its 60ft (18.3m) mast and long bowsprit, the bawley had a particularly large sail area. Because it fished from the Thames estuary it was designed to sit comfortably on the mud when the tide went out. Eventually they ranged from 28 to 37ft (8.5–11.3m).

Mistakenly thought to be slower than smacks, they had a slightly raked transom stern, plumb stem and straight keel with greatest draught aft. The Essex fishing smacks, with their sweeping, sheer, fine bows, counter stern and cutter-rig long topmast and bowsprit, had a style (and an ability to sail to windward) denied to most of their contemporaries. They were all-purpose boats used to trawl for bottom fish, dredge for oysters and scallops and sometimes for 'salvaging'.

Every species of fish, it seemed, demanded its own type of boat. In the fifty years leading up to the First World War, for instance, up to eighty special shrimpers around 20ft (6.1m) long worked from Yarmouth to supply the seemingly insatiable demand from late-Victorian holidaymakers for shrimps for their tea. But by the 1980s pollution from the Broads had wiped out the shrimp population and today only one of the old boats, romantically named *Horace and Hannah** remains in sailing order.

The fisherman's way of life, his boats, his tackle, nets and habits, depended on the kind of fish he was looking for and where. The Cornish oyster dredgers, confined to the peaceful waters of the Helford River, had very little in common with the Scots setting off from Aberdeen and Peterhead to fish for herring in the rough waters of the North Sea. But they shared the superstitions which abound in all fishing communities and indeed in other dangerous occupations. Many of these centred on the womenfolk. At Sennen in Cornwall, women were locked indoors when the fishermen went to sea, a habit which persisted until the 1920s.

Before the discovery of gas and oil in the North Sea, Aberdeen relied heavily on the fishing business. This photograph was taken in 1954 but could have been any time in the previous half-century.

Life on all of these boats, even when conditions were not dangerous, was always hard. Daniel George, born in 1877, told Jim Holmes, himself a veteran drifterman:

It was awful in the sailing boats... We didn't have a fo'c'sle, we had a cabin. When I was in the *Nellie Jabe* we always used to have two on a watch. The bunks weren't long enough so we had to knock the bulkhead down so a man could lay his head one way and his feet the other so our feet used to be close to each other, packed like sardines . . . There were bunks but not big enough to sit on . . . For cooking we had a stove down in the cabin, an open stove . . . There was no lavatory; we had to sit over the side, you'd go to leeward and catch hold of the rail or rigging, there was no bucket in those days . . . We didn't have much fresh water.[6]

The fishermen all had to be expert sailors, able to control their boats accurately – it is far easier to go fast in a yacht or schooner than to sail your fishing boat at exactly the right speed to be at the right place at the right moment. They had gaff rigging to help control the speed, but the large area of canvas demanded expert handling to set a precise speed, whatever the fishing method, longlining, trawling, or dredging.

While fishing methods, fish and boats differed widely between regions, many of them were linked in a seasonal migration, established in the mid-nineteenth century. In the early months of the year boats from East Anglia would descend on the Cornish port of Padstow, looking mainly for sole in the season when the plaice they fished in the North Sea were spawning. The biggest of these annual migrations was from Scotland to East Anglia, which is discussed later in this chapter. Both the coastal regions of East Anglia and Cornwall – the latter at least until tourists started to descend in large numbers in the second half of the nineteenth century – depended on fishing. As John Rowe explains, 'The sea has played a greater part in the life of Cornish people than the land in which they dwelt.'[7] The communities bred their own lore, habits and language; the Cornish, to a greater extent even than other seagoing communities, developed their own vocabulary. Fish baskets, for instance, were known as 'cowels' and the fishwives who carried them on their backs hawking fish among villages and farms far from the sea were 'jowsters'.

By the middle of the sixteenth century pilchards and hake, generally in pickled form, were being exported as far as the Mediterranean from Looe, and by the time Richard Carew published his Survey of Cornwall in 1602 Cornish fishing was of national importance. Carew's description of the seine net would be familiar to nineteenth- and indeed twentieth-century fishermen: 'The seine is a net about forty fathom in length with which they encompass a part of the sea, and draw the same on land by two ropes fastened at his ends, together with such fish as lighteth within his precinct'.[8] When the fishery was at its height, in the latter part of the nineteenth century, the nets were huge, at least a quarter of a mile (0.4km) long and 100ft (30.5m) deep.

Drift nets known as 'drovers' or 'drivers' created a permanent tension between the two. Carew records:

The seiners complain with open mouth that these drovers work much prejudice to the commonwealth of fishermen, and reap thereby small gain to themselves; for the taking of some few breaketh and scattereth the whole shoal and [discourages] them from approaching the shore; neither are those taken merchantable, by reason of their bruising in the mesh. Let the crafts-master decide the controversy.

There was a distinct contrast between the diamond-shaped seine net in which the fishermen hoped to catch mixed fish of high quality and 'purse seining', in which a wall of net surrounded the fish and was then pulled tight.

Fishing, at least as far as the east Cornish fleet was concerned, had four seasons, starting with crabbing, then mackerel fishing until June, when the boats were made ready for the pilchards in late autumn between harvest and Hallowe'en (as the local saying had it: 'When the corn is on the shock, then the fish are on the rock.'). Finally, with the onset of bad autumnal weather the fishermen would take to hand lines and fish for hake.

FOLKESTONE HARBOUR 5984.

Back in 1900, Folkestone was still a busy fishing port – note the small barrels of fish being landed.

The pilchard, a rarity now, and familiar even to the older generation only in tins, is a sort of mature sardine, and was for centuries a particular speciality of Cornish fishermen. Pilchard fishing started in Cornwall in the sixteenth century. Passing ships would report pilchards in two great shoals, north and south. They were caught by seine fishers (a seine involved three boats and two nets as well as a pilchard cellar), who were subject to legal prohibitions on breaking up the mass of fish before it reached the shore. 'Huers' would stand and watch. When the shoal came inshore the sea turned purple and screeching gulls would dive at the water, which 'boiled and rippled' with flashing silver (13 million fish were caught in a single seine net at St Ives in 1905). At this point the huers would cry 'Hevva!' through long tin trumpets to let the seiners know that the fish were in sight. They then directed the seiners using a simple semaphore system.

The granite cellars where the fish were cured with salt, a process called 'bulking', were known as 'pilchard palaces'.

One survives at the back of the beach at Penberth, where pilchard fishing stopped back in 1928. It still has in its stone floor the original groove into which the pilchard oil used to flow. The process did not change much in the centuries after Carew's description of it. The pilchards were 'first salted and piled up row by row in square heaps on the ground in some cellar, which they term bulking, where they remain for some ten days until the superfluous moisture of the blood and salt be soaked from them'. After they had been 'bulked' for a month, the fish were washed and pressed into barrels which held up to 2,500. The 'train oil', as it was known, was carefully kept and burned in a 'chill', a coarse pottery lamp which provided light for the locals' cottages.

Seine netting for pilchards peaked in the forty years after the Great Western Railway reached Cornwall after Brunel's great bridge over the Tamar west of Plymouth had been completed in 1859. This encouraged fishing for all types of pelagic fish – those that swim near the surface, such as pilchard, herring and mackerel. There was then a race to get the catch on to the London train to Billingsgate. Later, special steamers were used to get the fish from the fishing grounds, sometimes past the Scilly Isles, to Penzance. The railway had the effect of concentrating the industry, for small communities beyond the reach of the terminus could not compete with their more accessible neighbours, and above all with Newlyn.

The number of pilchard drivers increased at the end of the nineteenth century as drift netting became more common and beach seining declined – the drifters could reach the shoals further out to sea. Fish were frozen at sea, at first by using enormous chunks of Arctic ice and then, from about 1900, by freezing fresh water on the boat itself. Around 1910 luggers were being built as motor sailors and within a decade nearly all the boats were produced with engines. But, according to Dave Smart, 'As the drift net fishery increased and steam-powered trawlers made it possible to catch larger fish such as cod, ling, hake, conger and pollack, the pilchard seine-fishing industry was doomed.'[9] Early this century, as the pilchard became scarce – and could in any case be imported much more cheaply from West Africa – the locals changed to long lining for cod and skate. Nevertheless, a few years ago the Newlyn firm British Cured Pilchards was still sending pilchards to Italy.

The same cycle of boom and bust also affected mackerel fishing. In the late nineteenth century over 400 Cornish sailing drifters and 200 steam drifters went out to hunt the mackerel, more elusive than the pilchard. 'Mackerel will bite like hell,' says Don Turtle, a retired Newlyn fisherman, 'and then as soon as the tide turns, that's it, nothing.'[10] Stocks fell and by the 1930s the fishery had virtually closed down. But thirty years later a new breed of purse seiners, with huge nets wound on a drum paid out through a gantry on the vessel's stern, joined hundreds of smaller craft in the hunt for stocks which had naturally replenished themselves. Even the small boats, using lengths of line with fifteen feathers concealing hooks held over the side, managed to make a living from the newly fashionable appetite for mackerel, fresh, frozen, or

smoked. But this rebirth was short-lived: thanks largely to EC restrictions virtually all the 150 or so mackerel fishers active in the late 1970s had disappeared a decade later.

Boats from the east coast began to arrive in east Cornish sailing grounds in the 1860s and by 1878 about a hundred of them were fishing in south-western waters. They also created something of a social revolution: the locals were devout Methodists and would not fish on the Sabbath; the newcomers, less religiously inclined, worked on Sundays and thus established a monopoly on supplying fish for Monday-morning markets. In 1896 local resentment culminated in riots in Newlyn and Penzance which had to be suppressed by the army. These were not the only riots – the advent of steam drifters brought English fishermen into conflict, often bloody, with their Scottish brethren.

For nearly a century Yarmouth and Lowestoft were the centre of a major industry based on the seemingly inexhaustible shoals of herring in the North Sea. It was a world linked to its markets by railway – and by sea – but there were even closer links with the east coast of Scotland, source of the seasonal migration which followed the herring south. Jim Holmes records:

> When I was a boy Yarmouth was dominated by the herring industry . . . Early in the year we used to see certain boats preparing to go to Plymouth and Penzance, the 'westward' as they called it . . . Later some boats sailed northwards for the Scotch fishing. Many a time I've watched them steaming past Caister, Scratby and Winterton where some of the wives and sweethearts gave tearful little waves and the drifters hooted as they steamed away to fish the Minch, the Hebrides, Pentland Firth and other parts, gradually working their way home via Wick, Fraserburgh, Aberdeen, Shields, Scarborough, Grimsby and Dogger Bank, then back for the autumn fishing or 'home fishing', the main voyage of the year. This was the climax of the year's fishing and hundreds of English and particularly Scottish drifters converged on Yarmouth and Lowestoft, crowding the quays.

A quayside scene at Yarmouth in early October 1937, getting ready for the herring fishing season to open.

In the summer, the Scottish fishing fleet followed the herring round the coast of Scotland as far out as Barra in the Outer Hebrides.

Yarmouth was not the only fishing port on the east coast. Earlier in the season the migratory hordes of Scottish fisher girls worked at Scarborough, watched by panama-hatted holidaymakers.

The Scots' great prosperity came in the nineteenth century after they had learned what became known as the Scotch cure for herrings. This had in fact been invented by a Dutchman nearly five centuries earlier, and until well into the nineteenth century the Dutch were masters of the North Sea fishing grounds. But by the 1860s the men from Fife in particular were roaming the sea, migrating south in the autumn, able to land their catch at ports from Aberdeen south to Yarmouth, secure in the knowledge that the railways could carry the result to market in London.

The migration was twofold, consisting of both fishermen and the thousands of girls who gutted and packed the herrings. The world of North Sea herring depended on a wide variety of shore-based helpers. The nets were checked by the 'ransackers', and repaired by female 'beatsters'. Most of the girls were employed in preparing the fish. They worked in threes – two gutted and one packed – and were paid as a team. The 'gutter' flung the guts into a barrel, which was then carted away to be used for fertilizer. The herrings were sold in many different forms, but were generally smoked. The best known, kippers, were smoked according to a northern recipe brought to Yarmouth by a Newcastle man, John Woodger. They came in various types: the heavily smoked 'reds' and the 'golden herrings' were salted and then more lightly smoked for up to a fortnight; the 'silvers' salted and smoked for under a week. The famous Yarmouth bloater was invented by accident in the 1830s by a curer called Bishop, who left some herrings overnight in the smokehouse. The short period of cooking meant that they had been heated rather than heavily smoked so were best eaten fresh.

As in Cornwall, 1914 marked the end of a golden age for the fishing communities of East Anglia. The boom culmi-nated in what was known as the 'Klondyke trade', so called after the Alaskan gold rush at the end of the nineteenth century. 'It was actually started,' explains David Butcher, 'by a Lowestoft merchant called Benjamin S. Bradbeer who, while visiting friends in Hamburg during the year 1887, noticed just how great the German demand for fresh her-ring was.'[11] This demand was at the time satisfied largely by the Norwegians. Bradbeer promptly returned to Lowestoft and started to ship lightly salted herrings, particularly to the port of Altona. By 1914 there were 600 steam drifters regis-tered in Lowestoft and Great Yarmouth alone.

The herring business never fully recovered after the First World War. Foreigners couldn't afford herring, and if they could they built their own boats. The slump of the 1930s ended all hopes of a revival. Dennis George recalls that '1930 was the last year for making a profit . . . In Yarmouth and Lowestoft no end of owners lost every penny who in good times could have retired on £15,000 or £20,000 [over £500,000 today]. They lost everything.'[12] Between the late 1920s and 1939 the East Anglians lost the market for herring, and sometimes drifters would come into port after eight or nine hours' fishing and would then have to return to dump their catch at sea for want of buyers, despite periodic

attempts to control the market by imposing a quota system. The same decline could be seen in Cornwall. In 1889 the east Cornish fleet numbered 218 boats, but by 1936 the figure was down to 36, not one of them a sailing lugger. In East Anglia the decline was steady but remorseless, and by 1969 no herring boats arrived in Great Yarmouth at all. Fortunately, stocks have recovered somewhat after a total ban on herring fishing in the North Sea in the mid 1970s.

For all the fascination of Cornish and East Anglian fishing, it is Scotland that has always provided the biggest fishing fleet in the British Isles, for obvious reasons. It has far more coastline per inhabitant than England or Wales, and the country's small, far-flung maritime communities naturally relied on fishing, to the same extent as the Cornishmen but on a far larger scale.

The first Scottish fishing vessels were small open double-ended clinker-built rowing and sailing craft owing a lot to earlier Norse invaders. The combination of the industrial revolution – not only in Britain, for Germany and Russia were also large markets for Scottish fish – and the spread of the railways provided many Scots, particularly on the east coast, with opportunities which required larger vessels. These started with the scaffie, much favoured on the Moray Firth. Gloria Wilson describes this boat, with its tall, dipping lug sail, as 'clinker-planked and double-ended; she was full at the stern with steeply raked sternpost, curved stem and flat somewhat hollow floors and low bilges'.[13] The scaffie answered readily to the helm but was too full to be safe in a following wind. In the latter half of the century came the full development of what Wilson calls 'the famous decked east coast fifie, characterized by the almost vertical stem and sternpost . . . rigged with a huge high-peaked dipping lug sail and a standing lug mizen'.

The advantages of the two designs were married in the zulu, so named because the first was built in 1879, the year of a bloody campaign against the Zulus. 'With vertical stem and raked sternpost,' says Wilson, 'she had the handiness of the scaffie and the seakeeping qualities and weatherly capabilities of the fifie' – a combination repeated in hundreds of boats.

Around the turn of the century steam drifters – built at first in England and then in Scotland, albeit to English designs – began to impose themselves. Not surprisingly, the first steam-powered boats had been the longer-haul ones. In 1877 a Sunderland steam tug, the *Messenger*, was converted into a trawler. It was so successful that four years later the steam-powered *Zodiac* was launched in Grimsby. The conversion was rapid: by 1909 the national steam fishing fleet numbered 1,400 vessels, and three years later there were 800 steam vessels registered in Scotland alone. Steam power came later for drifters. The first steam drifter, the *Consolation*, was built in Lowestoft in 1898. They were wooden-hulled, up to 90ft (27.4m) long and less beamy than the sailing boats, but with deeper bulwarks.

The Cornish fishermen were slow to follow the example of their Scottish counterparts. Their first steam-powered fishing boat had been built at Hayle in 1876, but Newlyn had to wait a further thirty years for its first steam drifter. The fact that sail lasted longer in Cornwall than in Scotland and East Anglia sprang not so much from conservatism as from more severely practical considerations. The North Sea fishermen could get cheap coal from the Tyne, whereas the Cornish had to rely on coal brought (relatively) expensively from South Wales. In addition, a boiler and coal took up precious space which the Cornish sailors preferred to devote to fish.

Later, however, fishermen in both regions were ready enough to exploit internal combustion engines, first relatively primitive 'oil' engines and then diesels. The Scots in particular learned from the success of Danish motor boats between the wars – and not only in terms of their method of propulsion but also their fishing techniques: the Danes used seine nets to catch white fish, an approach which kept the Scots prosperous for several decades after the war. The Scots quickly switched to medium-sized fife-type motor boats, not only for seining but also to catch herring and shellfish. The novelty was compounded by the adoption of the rounded cruiser stern.

During the 1930s, says Wilson, 'Scottish yards built dozens of wooden-hulled cruiser-sterned diesel-engined seine net

Opposite: The Fish Wharf at Yarmouth in October 1937 witnessed a potential glut of herring from a boat with the endearing name of *Our Kate*.

The last scaffie built in the little Scottish fishing port of Avoch for a local firm, run by the Reid brothers. Avoch, on the Moray Firth opposite Inverness, is still a thriving fishing port.

vessels in the 50 to 60ft [15.2–18.3m] size range . . . Multicylinder diesel engines were relatively lightweight compared with earlier semidiesels and were also easier on fuel than paraffin engines.' British fishermen had the great advantage of the Gardner engine developed in the late 1920s and so reliable that it was used to tow into port boats powered by less sturdy units. By 1938 there were nearly 2,500 motor boats in the fleet compared with fewer than 750 steam-powered vessels. The remaining 1,848 sailing craft were mostly too small to be of real industrial importance. The cruiser-sterned wooden craft were wonderfully seaworthy. Wilson records how when the *Silver Chord* was off the Faroes, 'A sea rolled on to her starboard beam, and her wheelhouse touched the water, but she righted herself

The tradition continues: the *Floresco*, a wooden seiner-trawler, pictured at the tiny port of Pittenweem on the north bank of the Firth of Forth in 1973.

again. She also worked lines at Rockall, 200 miles [322km] west of the Outer Hebrides and known as the place where bad weather was invented.'

After the war the Scots adopted another Scandinavian technique: trawling for herring in twos or threes. Boats increased in depth, becoming fuller, and they also reverted to the transom stem. Fishing in Scotland flourished – in the early 1970s the catch increased by 100,000 tons to 475,000 tons and the value nearly tripled. Scottish fishing has, relatively speaking, survived in better shape than any other section of the industry. For defeat in the 'Cod War' with Iceland in the mid-1970s spelled the end of the former proud high-seas fleets of Grimsby and Hull, which had relied on fishing in Icelandic waters. Elsewhere, especially off the west coast of Britain, the European Union has allowed recklessly improvident fishermen from the Continent, particularly from Spain, into waters which had been the preserve of the locals since the Spanish Armada. Today Penberth in Cornwall houses only five or six boats which fish for lobster, crab, bass and mackerel but, in the repetition of a familar story, the bass, much prized by the French, are disappearing.

Don Turtle sums up the situation bluntly.

There used to be places of sanctuary for the fish, e.g., around wrecks etc., away from the hunters... Today the whole structure of the common market fisheries policy is flawed. It has been negotiated by people who are ignorant of fishing . . . There's no effective conservation policy . . . When the Spanish wanted a part of the EC fishery, every country had to cut down its fishing fleet by a certain amount. Because the Spanish already had a large number of vessels, they ended up with the lion's share. The Newlyn fishing fleet was reduced by a third – it had to, if it didn't, then it wouldn't get any EC assistance . . . Spain was allowed to modernize its fleet, Newlyn wasn't . . . The most modern boats in Newlyn are thirty years old . . . The Spanish target the small fish, the 'future stock' . . . Under EEC rules, the fishermen are only allowed to catch so much of one species per month, so fishermen are forced to throw good fish back. What's the point when they're dead anyway? . . . The British fishing industry is a natural gift: it doesn't require cultivation, it replenishes itself; if managed properly it could generate wealth and jobs . . . the Icelanders have their fisheries intact – fishing is three-quarters of their national production . . . We want to make our rules ourselves like them.

* It was built for one Horace Gedge and named either after him and his wife or for his mother and father.

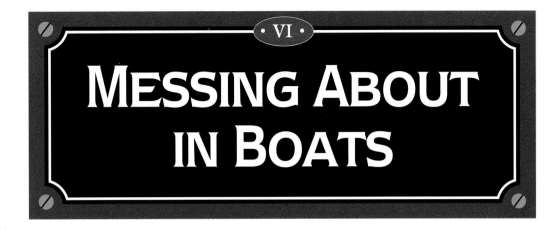

MESSING ABOUT IN BOATS

NEARLY NINETY YEARS AGO Kenneth Grahame provided the definitive distillation of the attraction of water as the ideal scene for 'leisure activity' (or inactivity). He put his definition into the mouth of Ratty in *The Wind in the Willows*: 'Believe me my young friend, there is *nothing* – absolutely nothing half so much worth doing as simply messing about in boats . . . In or out of 'em, it doesn't matter, that's the charm of it. Whether you get away, or whether you don't; whether you arrive at your destination or whether you reach somewhere else, or whether you never get anywhere at all, you're always busy, and you never do anything in particular; and when you've done it there's always something else to do, and you can do it if you like, but you'd much better not.'

Theses could be written on the deleterious influence of the idea of leisure on the British character, the lure of its apparent futility and purposelessness. But it remains deeply beguiling, an abiding relic of the seemingly endless, everlastingly sunlit afternoons of the summers that preceded the First World War. Sixty years earlier railways had given Londoners access to the Thames, on which they were able to capitalize more easily after the spread of the 'English weekend' which allowed clerical and managerial workers Saturday afternoons and Sundays off. The introduction of bank holidays in 1871 set the seal on what can only be called the great late-Victorian leisure revolution. This involved an unprecedented fashion for pursuits such as hiking and riding new-fangled bicycles.

Before the Great War, rivers, lakes and estuaries attracted far more than their fair share of this leisure activity. The rush to the water was greatly accelerated when King Edward VII commissioned a dream yacht, the *Britannia* (see Chapter 7) which his successor, George V, actually enjoyed sailing fast, especially in the roughest of weather. George V legitimized the increasing taste among the increasingly urbanized, increasingly sedentary British middle classes to take the next step: to stop messing about in boats and to tackle the elements. Indeed, it was Charles Nicholson, one of the greatest designers of ocean-going racing yachts, who initiated the idea of affordable 'one-design' yachts which could be produced in quantity. His Redwing design provided a unique testing ground for new technologies and sail settings, and it was followed by numerous imitators which played key roles in popularizing offshore – and international – sailing. (Two very different examples, the Golden Hind and the Fourteen and its charismatic promoter, Uffa Fox, are described in the features on pages 118 and 119).

Yet over the past century and a half most British watergoers have not been true sailors. Rather, they really do 'mess

Arthur Rackham does the impossible by providing the right image for Kenneth Grahame's *The Wind in the Willows*. Ratty and his new friend, Mole, were about to 'drop down the river together and make a long day of it'.

about in boats', propelled sometimes by sail, but more often by oar or engine. Britain's famous class distinctions were not dissolved in water: sailing, in particular, remained, if not exactly gentlemanly, certainly amateur. The two most famous races rowed on the Thames, Doggett's Coat and Badge, for professional watermen, and the University Boat Race, symbolized the two separate boating worlds. Bill Lindley, a veteran water man, recalled workers' outings sixty years ago.

> Practically every Sunday during the summer, you'd have the rowing clubs. They were the Globe, the Curlew, Poplar and Blackwall. All dockers and lightermen – mainly lightermen, though – rowing. And they'd have a regatta. Say four races. And they'd have the old steamer, the Royalty. These were old pleasureboats. And you'd have the bookmaker on there. And they'd start at ten on Sunday morning.[1]

What seemed 'a lovely day out' for Bill's wife Flo was hard work for a participant, Jack Woolenough. 'We used to race from Blackwall Tunnel to Wapping and then reverse as the tide was the other way. When you finished you'd had it, your arms were all limp. Of course, they were old boats. We'd have to row down to Blackwall first and by the time we got down there, we'd have to get out and bail the water out of the boat.' This sounds much tougher than the pace set by Jerome K. Jerome in his double-sculling skiff. He recounted:

> I pulled splendidly. I got well into a steady rhythmical swing. I put my arms, and my legs, and my back into it. I set myself a good, quick, dashing stroke and worked in really grand style . . . At the end of five minutes, I thought we ought to be pretty near the weir, and I looked up. We were under the bridge, in exactly the same spot that we were when I began . . . I let other people pull up backwaters against strong streams now.

Cosy-looking, unmistakably Victorian house boats on the Thames at Staines in 1895, when it was still a very rural stretch of river.

The adventures encountered by the author, and his fellow passengers George and Harris (not forgetting Montmorency the dog), made Jerome into one of the prime promoters of the pleasures of the river. His *Three Men in a Boat*, published in 1889, sold 200,000 copies in Britain alone, and over a million in pirated editions in the United States.

Thirty years later Arthur Ransome introduced generations of children to the delights of small-boat sailing and even made a contribution to a nascent feminism with his heroine Ruth, who changes her name to Nancy because pirates had to be 'ruth-less'. He was an unlikely missionary: a journalist and British spy in Russia during the Revolution – marrying Trotsky's secretary in the process. Before he went off into fantasy with books like *Missee Lee*, Ransome managed to initiate his hundreds of thousands of readers, old and young, into the fundamentals of small-boat design and handling, while in the meantime telling an excellent story. In his first book, *Swallows and Amazons*, he distinguishes clearly between the two boats. *Amazon*, the newer one, has a proper centre board, 'an iron keel that we can lower into the water when we are beating against the wind'. But one of the boys, 'Captain John', defends *Swallow*, which 'sails very well to windward, she has a keel about six inches deep, but it's there all the time, so that we don't have to have any centre-board case to get in the way inside her'.

But it was A.P. Herbert, campaigner, politician and greatly underestimated defender of the liberties of the subject, who was the patron saint of the cult of messing about in boats. In his autobiography he wrote: 'Water has been the big thing in my life (though wine has played a part), water, that gentle soft beautiful companion, that tough, terrifying, ugly villain.'[2] Shrewdly, he noted: 'One of the great virtues of water is that its pleasures do not depend on size.' A.P.H. lived for much of his life on a relatively narrow stretch of the Thames in Hammersmith, where he contrived to sail, to row and generally 'to mess about'. His feelings, and indeed those of the whole boating fraternity, were summed up in his much-anthologized poem, 'My Ship'.

In the summer of 1945 A.P.H. (Sir Alan Herbert) took his family on a demob cruise on his beloved *Water Gipsy*, which took three weeks to sail the sixty or so miles from Hammersmith, in west London, to Oxford.

My ship is my delight,
　　I made her, she is mine,
I built her trim and tight,
　　I dreamed her gracious line;
No wooden thing is she
　　But some proud part of me,
I made her she is mine.

Then at the helm I stand
　　And not alone are we,
Two lovers hand in hand,
　　We ask no company.
So, by some lover's art
　　I think she knows my heart
And sings or sighs with me.

In the early 1820s Londoners already used the Thames for pleasure trips downstream to Margate.

Opposite: Henley in 1994. Traditions – in the form of these immaculate skiffs – are properly maintained.

Cynical amateur psychologists could argue that such sentiments exposed messing about on the river as a typical attempt by the British middle-class male to escape from the complications involved in too close an association with the opposite sex (although A.P.H. himself was happily married for half a century). As a writer he leaped to fame in 1930 with the publication of his novel of canal life, *The Water Gipsies.* Not that he had much direct experience. His biographer, Reginald Pound, declared: 'He never went beyond the urban bounds, and for that reason his later elevation to the status of patron saint of the narrowboats was a mystery to some observers of that scene.'[3]

The boat bearing the name of the novel was Herbert's second. The first was a flat-bottomed 43ft (13.1m) barge with 'a tired and disloyal engine'. To A.P.H. it resembled Noah's Ark, and was so named. The *Ark*'s successor, the *Water Gipsy*, was equally unusual, in its owner's eyes, anyway. It was 'A queer, uncommon craft . . . with two nine horse-power petrol engines by Thornycroft.' It was very dear to him: even when

it was 'dead' he dreamed of it in 'some of the few dreams I wish were true when I wake up'. Generations of boat owners would undoubtedly echo his feelings.

A.P.H. used his new boat to commute (a term he thought absurd) to the House of Commons and found it relaxing after a hard day. He was a man of many parts, and his new revue *Home and Beauty* was in rehearsal at the same time as he was piloting through Parliament his bill to make divorce easier. 'I was nearly dotty between them. I would row out after the worrying day, climb aboard and light the lanterns and feel safe at last.' But he couldn't escape entirely. On his way home one Thursday evening, thinking, 'Thank God, no more divorce till Tuesday,' he was hailed by a voice from a passing tug whose owner had recognized his boat: 'You're doing no good. Bill wants to get rid of his old woman now.'

The Thames was Britain's only 'universal' waterway, where the three forms of power, sail, steam and, later, diesel co-existed, albeit uneasily. By contrast Windermere, the biggest stretch of water in the Lake District, was largely devoted to steam power ('It's like the bloody sea,' said one devotee of the Thames). England's other major 'leisure' waterway system, the Norfolk Broads, was devoted to sail power, if only because it is so breezy, with nothing to interrupt the north-east winds coming in, which it often feels, direct from Siberia.

Since the early nineteenth century the Thames estuary had been a favourite haunt of Londoners on an outing to Margate or Ramsgate on board a pleasure steamer. But the construction of the Great Western Railway past the bridge at Maidenhead, immortalized in Turner's 'Rain Steam and Speed', opened up the upper river. 'It was during the years 1880–1900,' wrote Reginald Bolland, 'that all the things we associate with the Victorian Thames flourished – houseboats and steam launches, regattas and Venetian fetes, river picnics and carnivals.'[4] The Thames became such a familiar playground that it was never referred to by its name, it was simply 'the river'.

The crowd was naturally at its thickest during the regatta at Henley at the beginning of July. The atmosphere was superbly captured by a contributor to *Punch*, quoted by Bolland, who called himself 'Jingle Junior' after the character in Dickens' *Pickwick Papers*.

All right – here we are – quite the waterman – jolly –
young – white flannels – straw hat – canvas shoes –
umbrella – mackintosh – provide against a rainy day!
Finest reach for rowing in England – best regatta in the
Eastern Hemisphere – finest picnic in the world!
Gorgeous barges, palatial houseboats – superb steam-
launches – skiffs – randans – punts – wherries – sailing-
boats – dinghies – canoes! . . . Towing path blocked up
with spectators – meadows alive with picnic parties –
flags flying everywhere – music – singers – niggers –
conjurors – fortune teller! Brilliant liveries of rowing
clubs – red – blue – yellow – green – purple – black –
white all jumbled up together – rainbow gone mad –
kaleidoscope with delirium tremens. Henley hospitality
proverbial – invitation to sixteen luncheons – accept
'em all – go to none. Find myself at luncheon where I
have not been asked – good plan – others in reserve!

Opposite: The Henley Regatta in 1893: rightly was it called the heyday of the Regatta, the Empire and the long Victorian summer afternoon, etc., etc.

The last of the line. The *Waverley*, the only sea-going paddle-steamer still steaming away in its natural habitat, passing under Erskine Bridge on the Clyde.

Food always played a large part in the hunger-inducing pastime of boating. Remember the list of the luncheon basket provided by Ratty in *The Wind in the Willows*: 'There's cold chicken inside it . . . coldtonguecoldhamcoldbeefpickledgherkinssaladfrenchrollscresssandwidgespottedmeatgingerbeerlemonadesodawater.'

Jingle Junior would have lunched on one of the countless houseboats lining the river. The interiors were classic examples of overstuffed Victorian domesticity; the exteriors, far more to modern taste, were hung with innumerable window boxes and pots full of flowers. The range of boats that actually moved was enormous, including types of craft the river had made peculiarly its own, like the slipper and the skiff. Bolland quotes from the 1883 edition of Dickens' *Dictionary of the Thames* – 'Pair-oared gigs, randan gigs, large shallop, large four-oared gigs with side seats, randan pleasure skiffs, pair-oared skiffs' – which, like that hired by Jerome K. Jerome's not-so-merry crew, could be supplied with tent covers and mattresses.

The well-covered skiff was also much used by courting couples anxious to keep away from prying eyes. Over the years it became less fashionable since rowing was increasingly transformed from a peaceful pastime into an energetic sport. This resulted in a compromise between a skiff and a dinghy. 'The Thames skiff may be ideal for the chap who's rowing it, because it is very easy to pull through the water, but it's not a boat that you can comfortably move about in,' says boat-builder Peter Freebody, who owns a yard in the village of Hurley near Maidenhead. 'So to gain stability, my grandfather developed a model with a wider transom. The boat was not flat-bottomed, but certainly flattened out in section, so it was more stable and comfortable.'[5]

Opposite: A steam-launch rally on Lake Windermere provides a lovely mix of retro-chic (as witnessed by the hats) and the decidedly modern chocolate biccies.

The Baby Greyhound slipper launch, still the ultimate in graceful waste of boat – especially if it's not used at its full 14-knot design speed.

The skiff evolved from the old Thames wherries, which were originally water taxis carrying passengers and loads of every description. But it remained 'commercial' when it was hired out, for profit or pleasure, as a gig or a pleasure skiff, in the boom of the last quarter of the nineteenth century. Many other types, and not only on the Thames, also developed from working boats, if only because these were the only models available. The most obvious examples are the adaptations of the Norfolk wherry (see page 77) and the punt. The punt is a type peculiar to the Thames (a 'Cornish punt' is a sailing dinghy) and was originally a flat-bottomed boat for moving gravel. When converted into a pleasure craft it became more luxurious, but the propulsion system (which is actually quite efficient, although it looks odd and ungainly in inexperienced hands) remained the same. The variety of powered boats was equally wide, from rowing boats with an outboard fixed on to the stern to the diesel-powered tourist boats and the 'floating gin palaces'. These came in all shapes – there were, and are, even launches designed specially to carry the umpires for the many boat races held on the river.

Over the years designs drifted further and further away from their humble origins. The most obvious case was the use of the clipper bow on powered launches. They had no need of a bowsprit, but it was added because it looked so elegant. By the 1930s 'design' had become a crucial factor. Gibbs of Teddington built lovely traditional transom-sterned launches and Taylor and Bates made even more stunning beaver-tailed examples. But they were more complicated to build than the uncrowned king of the Thames, the 'slipper' launch, which, in its early days, was simply nailed together.

This launch dates back to 1912 and the introduction of the first petrol engine, from America, on the river by an enterprising nineteen-year-old from a boatbuilding family, John Andrews. The design took off in the 1920s and Andrews introduced the classic design, the Greyhound, powered by the marine version of an Austin engine. The most extravagant of them all was the 50ft (15.24m) long Baby Greyhound. Appropriately enough, the design had a renaissance in another decade dedicated to *la bella figura*, the 1980s. Its leading contemporary proponent, Peter Freebody, admits that: 'It is decadence . . . the lines are wasteful, the long sweep of the stern serving no practical purpose except being a very beautiful way of creating a stern. Two-thirds of the foredeck accommodates very little but air.' But, he adds, 'It's also a very sensual boat,' and he has been 'asked by clients to put extra length into the forward hull "just to make it look more sexy" . . . There's no more beautiful way to end a boat.' It could also reach 14 knots, although few owners were speed freaks.

Freebody lovingly builds and rebuilds the slippers with mahogany keels between chines of Colombian pine and single planks of African mahogany for the sides. But then, boatbuilding is in his blood. The Upper Thames has been a home for boatbuilders for centuries, and he can trace his family back to 1257, when they were in business as ferrymen in nearby Caversham. They have been building boats for the past two centuries. He naturally prefers wooden boats because they are individual, unlike boats 'poured out of a 40-gallon drum' of plastic. Inevitably, therefore, his customers are 'the best people to work for – people with money to waste'.

The very different nautical habits on the Cumbrian lakes as opposed to the Thames are a prime illustration of the gulf between the cultures of northern and southern England. They had one common feature: both had become accessible with the construction of railways (although the railway didn't actually reach Windermere itself – William Wordsworth uttered a prototypical Nimby-type protest and the local landowner demanded too much money). Windermere was less elegant than the Thames. It featured chauffeured steam launches for the mill owners and coal magnates from Liverpool, Manchester and the cotton towns to the north, who had their country houses round the lake. They even used their boats on shopping trips as well as for pleasure. Bowness Bay in particular was viewed as the British equivalent of that most elegant of American resorts, Newport in Rhode Island.

The boating bug bit early in the Lake District – indeed, the Windermere Steam Boat Museum houses *Dolly*, built in 1850 and one of the oldest mechanically driven ships in the world still afloat. Status was demonstrated not only by the size, power and luxury of the family boat but extended even to the hats worn: the head of the family was instantly recognizable by his top hat, the son would have his boater, the ladies the latest creations, while the engineer wore a peaked cap. The engineer himself had a certain standing – indeed, the *Shamrock*, a steam launch built in 1906, was left by its original owner to his engineer. Unfortunately, after being passed down through his family it was eventually abandoned, to be rescued in the nick of time when about to be used as fuel on bonfire night in 1976. Now, happily, it has been restored. Another, the *Lady Hamilton*, was bought by some local grandees, the Sandys family of Graithwaite Hall, in 1929, and was invariably driven by the family's chauffeur. In the Second World War it was painted grey and formed part of a fleet of 'Dad's Navy' boats which guarded a factory making Sunderland flying boats.

The standard Windermere motor launch had a cabin with a raised roof in the middle section and an open front which offered better head room and cover (one Thames boatbuilder said firmly that he and his brethren 'would never ruin the line in such a way, even though it's obviously practical'.[6] But then, Thames builders always aimed for 'understated elegance'.) Windermere was roomy enough for races, and the locals were decidedly competitive. Some of the steam-driven boats were quick enough – the *Otto*, built in 1896, could do 18mph (30kph) and a sister boat reached 25mph (40kph). But it was not until the arrival of petrol engines that racing took off in earnest. The first power-boat race on Windermere, in 1925, involving members of the

A restorer's delight: a Severn Trow, called appropriately enough *Severn Collier*, one of many such wrecks lying on Britain's riverbanks.

Manchester Cotton and Stock Exchange, set the tone. Since then the Windermere Motor Boat Racing Club has actively promoted the sport. Local designers then took up the design of the winner, generally using engines from First World War warplanes. They sounded pretty terrifying, and the *Canfly*, equipped with a surplus Rolls Royce engine originally used in an airship, had no means of stopping except naturally. Racing became popular again in the 1950s – even the tragic death of Sir Donald Campbell in his attempt on the world water-speed record on nearby Coniston Water in 1959 did not temper enthusiasm. The face of power in the 1960s was the 28ft (8.5m) long Fairey Huntsman and the 40ft (12.2m) Nelson 40, designed by Commander Peter Thornycroft, which was so businesslike that it was adopted by harbour and water police authorities the world over. This was a far cry from Jerome K. Jerome, Mole, or indeed Arthur Ransome, who set his first books on the Lakes. But then, every proper stretch of waterway has room for both Ratty and Mr Toad.

QUITE A NUMBER of designs have become famous as sturdy, reliable family cruisers, but none was more beloved than the Golden Hind. It arrived on the scene in 1965 thanks to Hartwell's, a Plymouth-based joinery firm which specialized in 'funeral appointments' – coffins, in other words. The Golden Hind soon acquired such a high reputation that it was dubbed 'the Morris Minor of the yachting world' by one yachting journalist.

Hartwell's commissioned a well-known designer, Maurice Griffiths, who was already responsible for the Eventide and Waterwitch designs. He stuck to their basic features: a hard-chined bilge-keeler with transom-hung rudder, curved stem, high topsides, sweeping sheer, and a central ballast keel with twin steel bilge plates. The result was named after the boat made famous by another Plymouth man, Sir Francis Drake. In the words of Angus Macdonald, the new design 'soon established a reputation as a safe, roomy, family cruising boat, robust enough to cope with ocean passage-making, yet homely enough – with its three keels – to dump on the sand at journey's end'.[7]

Hartwell's built some 120 Hinds in the next five years before Terry Erskine, their yard manager, took over, set himself up in larger premises and built another 130. Over the years, of course, the design changed. They were originally built in marine plywood sheathed in resin, but Erskine switched to glassfibre and the boat was lengthened to provide more space below. The design's fame soon spread, and a number of American and Canadian buyers sailed their purchases home (in all, Hinds have clocked up a record forty-eight transatlantic voyages). In 1994 Mark Urry, an enthusiastic Hind owner, bought up the moulds and set up in business to manufacture them once more.

The design remains a classic combination of old and new: isophthalic resins, and an unashamedly high-tech cutter rig for 'light airs' sailing are combined with the use of plenty of hardwood in the cabin. When Urry abandoned the 5ft (1.5m) laminated tiller, the result, according to Macdonald, was that 'The boat glides on unperturbed, disdainful of anything so crude as a hand on the helm.'

Golden Hind: combining comfort and excitement for the amateur sailor.

UFFA FOX, larger-than-life character and one of the Duke of Edinburgh's few close friends, was also one of the rare geniuses in the history of small-boat design. He enabled thousands of sailors throughout the world to enjoy sailing of a speed and sophistication previously available only to the lucky rich.

Fox was not the first to design for the masses. He himself praised as 'a sound, sensible, sturdy and seamanlike little vessel' the X-boat, designed as far back as 1909 by Alfred Westmacott, and still growing in numbers. Even the design he revolutionized, the Fourteen, was not new. The first had been an amalgam of a large number of dinghies of 14ft (4.3m) which had been racing in different parts of the country as early as the turn of the century, notably the Norfolk dinghy and the West of England Conference dinghies. Standardization was further boosted after the First World War when the Boat Racing Association merged with the Yacht Racing Association. Its specifications (apart from being 14ft/4.28m long at the waterline) were that the rig had to be 125sq ft (11.6sq m), its weight 225lb (102kg); it could not have any inside ballast, and the sail plan could only be 22ft 6in (6.9m) above the gunwale, though the mast could be made in any way you liked.

When Fox was growing up on the Isle of Wight, the best Fourteens were designed by Frank Morgan Giles, who had a boatyard near Hammersmith Bridge in west London. Then came Fox's *Avenger*, which, as his biographer puts it, 'introduced a new dimension to yacht design . . . in one set of lines he had doubled the speed a dinghy helmsman could expect from his craft'.[8] The formula was simple, and owed a lot to Fox's seven-year apprenticeship

Uffa Fox and Prince Philip with a clearly unhappy nine-year-old Prince Charles.

with the S.E. Saunders company, best known for its flying boats. *Avenger* planed through the surface of the water thanks to its V-shaped sections. 'In the same way,' wrote his biographer, 'that a water skier places his skis at an angle to the water to give the lift required, so it is with a planing boat. Uffa likened it to a wedge of ice which, if pinched, jumps up and out of the fingers.' The new design won every race for which it entered.

Fox was not the only revolutionary of his time, either. The 1920s also saw the development of the Genoa jib by the great Swedish yachtsman Sven Salin, the first yachtsman to appreciate the advantage of a double-sided or parachute spinnaker for ease of gybing.

After the war, during which Fox designed an airborne lifeboat which saved hundreds of airmen's lives, he went on to design the Flying

Fifteen, dreamed up in his bath after his friends had pleaded with him to build a planing boat that would not capsize. This was so successful that he went on to design a whole 'Flying Family' in increasing lengths of 5ft (1.5m) a time.

In his last years Fox was best known as a friend of the Duke of Edinburgh, who contributed an introduction to Fox's biography. He described his friend as a man whose whole life 'was one long campaign against the foolish, the stupid and self-important, the whole conducted with a cheerful breeziness that disarmed all but the hardest cases', who may well have included two embittered ex-wives. The admiration was mutual, for Fox called the Duke 'a most wonderful boat sailor . . . able to take a boat to windward as well as anyone as I have ever met on this earth', and declared that he had an 'ability at everything he gives his heart to'.

Lake Windermere in the 1960s: the timelessness of leisure boating – and such an impression of space.

SAIL, SEA, SNOBBERY – AND TRUE GRIT

BIG YACHTS are not for the poor and wretched of this earth, they are for royalty, and lesser millionaires, to disport themselves, to consume conspicuously, to compete, to keep up with other titled and wealthy folk – and, in some cases, to enjoy themselves actually sailing. Appropriately enough, the idea of sailing yachts for pleasure was introduced in Britain by that supreme hedonist King Charles II, the spark for so many other elements of English civilization, from the consumption of fine wines and spirits such as port and champagne to the worship of well-bred spaniels, most particularly those named after him.

Charles was not, however, the first monarch to make merry on water. Half a millennium earlier King Edgar enjoyed 'sommer progresses and [his] yerely chiefe pastimes were the sailing round about this whole isle of Albion'. Charles got the idea from the Dutch, who can legitimately claim to be its inventors. 'Yacht' comes from their word *jaght*, meaning 'hunting' or 'chasing', and they were racing *jaghts* in the early 1600s, before they acquainted the exiled King with the joys of the sport. They even gave him a 52ft (15.85m) sloop, which was used for the first purely recreational yacht race in England, run from Greenwich to Gravesend.

It was the Dutch, too, who as settlers, had founded the longest-surviving traditional home of the schooner, in Gloucester, Massachusetts. The first boat to carry the innovative triangular headsail that has marked them out ever since was built there in 1713. According to E.K. Chatterton, the schooner got its name when someone remarked, 'Oh, how she scoons' – skims over the water – as she was leaving the stocks.[1] Over the next century and a half builders refined the idea, replacing the two-masted *sloepe* with a single foremast steeped very far forward, the better to carry fish from the Grand Banks off Newfoundland back to port as quickly as possible. By the end of the century, Chatterton remarks, 'Many of these Gloucester schooners were far more entitled to be called yachts than any other name.'

On the other side of the Atlantic, the first domestic yacht club, the still-thriving Royal Cork Yacht Club, was founded in the eighteenth century. The end of the Napoleonic Wars triggered a renewed interest, including the formation of today's Royal Yacht Squadron, which established its first race (for a gold cup valued at £100) in 1826 and set another, less sporting, tradition by providing that a mere two blackballs would make a candidate ineligible for membership.

It was Queen Victoria who unwittingly instituted the division between luxury and racing yachts. She disliked sailing and had two 300ft paddle-steamers built for her personal use, their interiors designed by dear Albert himself. Her decision separated the 'cruisers' from the true sailors. They immediately faced a challenge from the *America*, probably the most famous yacht in racing history. Based on the schooners built in Massachusetts, it was long and lean, lacking the 'cod's

Shamrock V, Sir Thomas Lipton's last challenger for the America's Cup. Before the days of powered winches, sailing such a monster was a hard and labour-intensive business.

head and mackerel tail' characteristic of its British contemporaries. Among its other innovations were sails made of cotton, rather than the British flax, sails which were laced to the spars, whereas those carried by English yachts were mere windbags, loose-footed on the boom. Its success was immediate: Donald M. Street records that one pilot was 'asked to heave the log himself as he would not believe that she was doing 12 knots with such a smooth wake'.[2] British yachtsmen were so frightened by her that they wouldn't race her until *The Times* taunted them to take her on. The *America* won the resulting competition round the Isle of Wight so convincingly that when Queen Victoria asked who had come second they replied: 'Your Majesty, there is no second.' Thus began the tradition epitomized by the race named after the yacht, the America's Cup. Britain has never won it.

The mid-nineteenth-century yachts were formidable affairs. Lord Brassey's *Sunbeam* was once timed at 15 knots and covered 299 miles (481km) in a twenty-four-hour period. Although scientists soon became involved, especially in studying the flow of water along the hull, it was an outsider, E.H. Bentall, an Essex agricultural implement maker, who in 1875 revolutionized yacht design with the *Jullanar*. The vessel was based on the obvious precept that length meant speed, and that a deep draught would provide the necessary stability. She was the first yacht to break from the naval traditions that had previously dominated yacht design. With her clipper bow and canoe stern she was originally regarded as rather ugly, and subsequent designs tended to reflect an obsession with length, encouraged by rules which levied taxes only on the length of a yacht at the waterline and on its sail area, thus precipitating the use of extravagant overhangs.

The history of the first golden age of competitive ocean racing, between the 1890s and the outbreak of the Second World War, centres around the royal yacht *Britannia*. Over the following forty years she was a supreme example of the mix of class, money and technology that made up the world of international yacht racing, then as now. The upsurge in interest was reinforced by Joshua Slocum, who completed the first single-handed round-the-world voyage in 1898, and

two years later yachting was introduced as a sport in the second modern Olympic Games. The era also produced the early ocean races, like the Bermuda Race, first sailed in 1906.

The first *Britannia* was a sailing ship, unlike the present vessel of that name. According to Anthony Heckstall-Smith, the then Prince of Wales, later King Edward VII, had her built in 1893 because the previous year his nephew, Kaiser Wilhelm II, had bought the cutter *Thistle* with the clear intention of competing in sailing as well as in more warlike naval construction.[3] Three years later, the Kaiser upped the stakes by building the great cutter *Meteor*, which was larger and had more sail than *Britannia*. He also encouraged his richer subjects to build and race yachts. One, *Germania*, was financed by Dr Krupp von Bohlen, who had it built in his own shipyard. The royal rivalry produced some nasty incidents which culminated in a row in 1907, after which peace was declared.

Britannia was a 2,111-tonner with a 110ft (33.5m) mast and was 102ft (31m) long. Manoeuvring her 10,000sq ft (929sq m) of sail was a labour-intensive business – in one illustration we can see the mainsail being launched by fourteen straining pairs of hands, including those of the ship's cook. To raise the topsail the crew climbed up the ratlines and crossed over to swing on the halyard, using their weight to add to that of the fifteen men on the deck. She was an immediate success. In her first season she beat the American champion *Navahoe* in four out of five races. She just lost once – and then only after a protest – after a race across the Channel during which the two were never more than 450ft (137m) apart. In 1895 she won a record thirty-three first prizes out of thirty-nine starts. By her last season, 1935, she had won 200 first prizes, still an unbeaten record.

More controversially, *Britannia* was at the centre of a series of confrontations which forced designers to deal with new rules. She ushered in the modern age of racing yachts in which increasingly tight regulations force designers into devising yet more ingenious and sophisticated designs, a precursor of the similar battle which has dominated motor racing over the past half-century. And, as we saw in Chapter 6, she inspired an obsession with racing yachts which had long-lasting repercussions, in

King George V at the helm of his beloved yacht Britannia in 1921. He really did enjoy sailing, especially in the roughest of seas, delighting in the seasickness suffered by many of his guests, including Queen Mary.

Opposite: The launch of Lipton's *Shamrock III* in 1903 – note the Shamrock flag and the rather ramshackle boatyard.

Sir Thomas Lipton in 1930 just before he died. Never a keen sailor, he nevertheless fully exploited the publicity provided by the sport for his tea business.

Competition meant continuous progress – *Britannia* had no fewer than seven different rigs in its forty-four-year life. One major innovation was the Marconi rig, a topmast that was stepped inside the mainmast and supported by cross-trees and stays, which saved a lot of unnecessary weight aloft. According to Heckstall-Smith, it was named after the inventor of radio signalling. When someone asked the reason for the wires and struts involved, a joker replied, 'They are part of her Marconi, carried so that she can signal for more whisky when the supplies run out.' More seriously, its adoption led directly to the simple, elegant Bermuda rig which eliminates any square sails at all. This was much simpler than the gaff rig it replaced, halving the time required to prepare for a race. Indeed, the abandonment of the gaff rig was as revolutionary a step as the supplanting of square rigging by the fore-and-aft, and provided the same sort of quantum leap when sailing close to the wind.

Public interest in big boats was such that Sir Thomas Lipton, Britain's greatest grocer, built a series of five yachts, all named *Shamrock*, to compete in the America's Cup. Heckstall-Smith says that his motive was not primarily sporting, that it was all 'a part of a great advertising campaign to sell Lipton's Tea . . . Tommy's repeated attempts to win the America's Cup were virtually the finest advertising stunts the world has ever known'. Whatever his motives, the challenge was serious enough: *Shamrock IV* might have won the America's Cup in 1914 had the race not been cancelled on the outbreak of war. Others seeking to acquire social respectability through the ownership of large yachts were less fortunate: at least two went broke, one of whom, Charles Hatry, went to jail for fraud.

Serious ocean racing resumed only in 1921, three years after the end of the First World War. Later in the decade came the arrival of the J-class[*], the most beautiful breed of racing yachts ever built – every boat, they said, wanted to be a J-class when it grew up. Like so many other rebirths, the J-class emerged as a result of changes in the rules, which prompted designs containing many echoes of the by-then thirty-year-old *Britannia*. The Js were enormous. They were between 76 and 87ft (23.2–26.5m) long at the waterline. Their masts reached over

Britain as well as abroad, in giving a royal seal of approval to the whole idea of racing in yachts, small and large.

Royal involvement became more serious when George V, a serious sailor uninterested in the sexual and social life at Cowes that had attracted his father, came to the throne. He employed Sir Philip Hunloke, reckoned to be one of the finest amateur helmsmen in the world, who was expected to drive the yacht to the limit of its powers, especially in bad weather (it was, supremely, a bad-weather yacht). Such instructions were a nightmare, for they obliged him to put the King – as well as his relations and other assorted monarchs such as the sailing-mad King Alphonso XIII of Spain – in danger of drowning.

The most magnificent spectacle in racing history: the J- class in full sail. From the left are *Uelsheda, Candida, Shamrock, Astra* and King George V's famous yacht *Britannia*.

Sir Thomas Sopwith's *Endeavour I* just ahead of *Britannia* before the ill-fated America's Cup which *Endeavour I* should have won.

160ft (48.8m), their mainsails weighed a ton, their flying jib alone was the size of the mainsail of a 39ft (12m) boat and their parachute spinnakers measured up to 18,000sq ft (1,672sq m).

Only ten J-class yachts were ever built, although a number of other 'big yachts' were adapted to the new rig, and they raced for a mere eight years, between 1930 and 1937. But, in a decade marked by the slump, they allowed lesser mortals to dream of a truly glamorous lifestyle. So it was natural for them to inspire the sort of interest otherwise devoted to the Hollywood stars who were the true rivals to the J-class for the attentions of the popular press.

The type came about as a result of negotiations over Lipton's fifth and last challenge for the America's Cup. As always, the pressure came from the Americans. As Junius Morgan of the New York Yacht Club put it: 'We look towards progress in design. The Europeans seem to wish to crystallize design with a view to retaining the racing life of a boat for the longest period of time.'[4] This attitude naturally led to European accusations that the Americans were interested only in built-in obsolescence. This was always rather unfair – in 1962 the *Nina*, built in 1928, skippered by a seventy-four-year-old, the magnificently named De Courney Fales, won the Bermuda Race.

Lipton agreed that *Shamrock V* would be a J-class, built to the American Universal Rule, which was easier to apply than the International Rule then in force. These regulations were hideously complicated: broadly, whereas under the International Rule an increase in length meant a corresponding and appreciable reduction in the area under sail, according to the Universal Rule, the waterline could be increased with hardly any penalty for sail area, providing only that the displacement was also increased, thus allowing far greater variety than had previously been possible. Following Lipton's acceptance of the American challenge, George V gave the class his blessing by engaging Charles Nicholson to carry out the necessary changes to *Britannia*'s spars and sails to enable the old boat to compete. The result, says Heckstall-Smith, was that she went 'like a scalded cat'.

The J-class took their place in what was called 'the big class' of yachts, like *Britannia*, built before 1930. They were

A colourful fleet of Ultra 30s, pictured at Southampton during the 1994 Ultra Yacht Circuit round the south coast of Britain.

immensely expensive to build – the Americans even used a special type of bronze, an extravagantly costly metal, for the seven they produced. Not only did these boats cost a fortune to construct and race, but they were fairweather vessels – the masts and rigging were so highly stressed that they simply could not cope with high winds. However, once underway their momentum could carry them for miles, even if there was scarcely any wind. Their inability to manage bad weather encouraged the spread of the smaller 39ft (12m) yachts which could sail in the roughest of conditions. The first 12m was the *Vanity*, built in 1922 according to what became known as the Second International Rule.

The high spots of racing in the mid-1930s were the challenges to the Americans by *Endeavour* and *Endeavour II*, both designed by Charles Nicholson and owned and raced by Sir Tom Sopwith, who had bought *Shamrock V* after Lipton's death. In the 1934 series *Endeavour* should have beaten the American challenger *Rainbow*, entered by Harold Vanderbilt, gambler and the inventor of modern contract bridge. But although Sopwith was one of a new breed of owners, an aircraft magnate who introduced many mechanical and electrical innovations and who understood aerodynamics and metal fatigue, he unfortunately retained the feudal attitudes of the previous generation. So when his professional crew walked out in protest at the inadequacy of their pay, he sacked them and replaced them with amateurs. In fact, his rival also had trouble with his crew, but he was more tactful. Sopwith was also accused of relying too heavily on his mechanical aids rather than on flair and instinct – 'When is Mr Sopwith going to sail his ship?' was the blunt comment of Nat Herreshoff, doyen of American yacht designers.

Even so, Sopwith might still have won but for an incident in the third race** which so unnerved him that he virtually collapsed in the rest of the series. Such was the attention paid to the races that the incident became an international *cause célèbre*, producing the memorable headline: 'BRITANNIA RULES THE WAVES – But America waives the rules.'

Unfortunately, Nicholson had generously allowed the Americans to see the actual lines of the first *Endeavour* and in 1937 a new yacht, *Ranger*, easily beat *Endeavour II*.

The J-class was a dream which couldn't last. The yachts proved too fragile and too expensive to maintain in the slump of the 1930s. *Britannia's* last great season was in 1931. Five years later she was scuttled in mysterious circumstances on the orders of the new King Edward VIII, who preferred golf to the sea. This act of philistinism and filial impiety set a symbolic seal on the era. By the outbreak of war only four J-class yachts were racing.

The obsession with the big class left its mark further down the size – and expense – scale. This can be seen in the story of the Fastnet Race, a race from Cowes to Plymouth via the famous rock off the southern Irish coast. This had been inaugurated by the Ocean Racing Club in 1925, and for its first

Class 1 Ocean Racers can never be built in a hurry: here are three under construction in 1958 at Groves and Gutteridge's boatyard at Cowes.

three years it was the club's only fixture. By 1937 the number of events had increased to eight and the Fastnet had changed beyond recognition, becoming truly international. By 1939 it had been divided into three divisions, Open, A and B, characterized in horsey fashion as for 'steeplechasers', 'genuine hunters' and 'cobs'. As Ian Dear relates, 'In other words, B Division was for the real old hookers, or "clumbungies", as they were described in the yachting press. Only one started that year and it did not finish.'[5]

The story of ocean racing since 1945 has been typical of most glamorous sports, comparable, as before the Second World War, with motor racing in particular. Races have become more numerous, amateurs have been largely replaced by professionals, and participation is now concentrated on companies able to afford the ever-escalating costs, sometimes as individual sponsors in their own right (like the late Baron Bich of Bic fame). The America's Cup continues as the most glamorous race, and the Fastnet is arguably the

The strangely-named Nioulargue Regatta for classic yachts held at Saint Tropez in 1994.

most popular (the entrants, a mere 100 yachts in 1971, had swelled to three times that number by the end of the decade). There are other successful newcomers, like the big race of the Cowes Regatta, the Admiral's Cup, introduced in 1957, and the Sydney–Hobart race. The toughest must surely be the Whitbread Round-the-World race, first sailed in 1973, in which each 7,000-mile (11,265km) leg is equivalent to two years' hard sailing on the Solent.

Traditionalists (and what yachting enthusiast is not susceptible to the appeal of the past after a couple of drinks?) will argue that racing has not been the same since the demise of wood, largely due to the introduction of glass-reinforced plastic in the 1960s. This change to synthetic materials had spread to sails, which are now made of kevlar, although old-established sailmakers like Ratsey and Lapthawn of Cowes, which dates back to 1790, use modern materials dyed to resemble the historic Egyptian cotton. In the same way sheets and halyards are coloured to look like the original hemp.

Now we have light, flexible multispreader rigs, multifunction hydraulics, and computer-designed, precision-shaped composite sails. Indeed, sail production is as computerized as any other piece of engineering – 'Sailmaking is engineering with cloth,' as one writer put it. Navigation bristles with the latest electronic gadgetry: the Decca navigator for continuous position finding and SATNAve satellite linked to an on-board computer for the real-time information on tide and wind. Hulls are constructed from new, exotic materials, all created to enable the racing machine to respond to the smallest change in the strength or direction of the wind. But whatever the materials, however packed the boats with computerized aids, the vessels themselves remain great design objects, still and forever dependent on the power and fury of the world's winds and waves.

Black Magic (skippered by Peter Blake) the New Zealand winner of the 1995 America's Cup, and the US loser, *Stars and Stripes* (skippered by Dennis Connor).

* The letter was one of a series of classes of yachts of different sizes from A to Q.

** Shortly after rounding the first mark, with *Endeavour* in the lead, Sopwith took the mark too wide, thus allowing Vanderbilt to hail out on to his weather. Inevitably this manoeuvre ended in a luffing match, during which Sopwith maintained he was obliged to bear away to avoid a collision with the defender *Rainbow*, whose duty, as overtaking boat, was to keep clear.

GLOSSARY –
or should it be gl'ss'ry?

Pace T.S. Eliot, the naming of ships is a far more serious matter than trying to fit a name, or names, to a cat. Outsiders are invariably humbled by the freedom with which nautical folk use esoteric words. They should not take their inferiority too seriously. As C.R. Benstead put it in a memorable passage:

There is nothing quite so bewildering, and infuriating, as the sailor's habit of calling different things by the same name when he is not calling the same things by different names . . . However much the sailor may succeed in mystifying, there are basically only two types of rig, one athwartships and called 'square', and the other fore-and-aft and so called . . . Vessels which combine the two rigs are also simple enough until the sailor tires of their simplicity. Take a ship; put fore-and-aft on her mizen and you have a barque. Put fore-and-aft on her mainmast as well and you have a barquentine. Now take a barque, and for economy's sake, denude her of such lofty drapery as skys'ls, roy'ls and even t'g'll'nts (the sailor has ever had a remarkable flair for talking in consonants punctuated by an occasional sneeze); do that, and she is said to be bald-headed – which does not seem unreasonable. When, however, you take a brig, step a small trysail mast immediately abaft the mainmast – so close indeed that it is almost touching – and then add that trys'l, or if so inclined, a spanker or gaff-mains'l, you have, unexpectedly, a snow, and pardonably wonder why. Fortunately the last of this enigmatic breed, the *Commerce* of Newhaven, melted away in 1909 at the not inconsiderable age of forty-seven.[1]

Barque Ship with three or more masts, only the one furthest aft is rigged fore and aft.

Bawley Type of cutter widely used in the Thames estuary.

Barquentine Square-rigged on foremast only, fore-and-aft-rigged on all other masts.

Bermuda rig Pure fore-and-aft rig, now universally made for racing yachts of all types.

Boom A long spar run out to extend the foot of a sail.

Brig (formerly brigantine) Ship with two masts, both square-rigged.

Carvel-built Boat with its planks fitting each other.

Clinker-built Boat with overlapping planks.

Clipper Full-rigged sailing ship.

Cutter Small vessel with single mast, fore-and-aft sails.

Fore-and-aft-rigged The sails when at rest lie in a line running from the bow to the stern. See **Square-rigged**.

Full-rigged ship Ship with between three and five masts, all set with square sails.

Gaff spar Used to extend the heads of sails that are not stayed.

Gybe When a ship alters course so that the wind comes from the opposite quarter, the mainsail of a ship which is rigger fore and aft will have swung over and will be said to have 'gybed'.

Halyard A rope or tackle used for hoisting or lowering sails and spars.

Ketch See **Yawl**.

Knots Ship's speed expressed in nautical miles, which equal 1.15 ordinary miles.

Lateen A long, triangular sail bent to a long yard, a characteristic sail of the Mediterranean and of dhow-rigger craft.

Leeward The direction away from the direction of the wind. See **Windward**.

Luff Sailing a ship close to the wind.

Masts The one nearest the bow is the foremast, the second typically the mainmast, and the furthest aft is the mizen-mast.

Mizen (or mizzen) The furthest aft mast of a vessel which has two or more masts.

Spinnaker Light, triangular-shaped sail set on the side opposite to that on which the mainsail extends, and used when running before the wind.

Spritsails In fore-and-aft ships the sprit is a spar used for stretching the peak of the sail, thus extending diagonally across the mast (used, for instance, in Thames barges).

Square-rigged The sails hang across the ship and are more or less rectangular in shape. See **Fore-and-aft-rigged**.

Tonnage All space enclosed within the hull. Net or registered tonnage excludes spaces not used forcarriage of passengers or cargo. Deadweight tonnage is that of a ship which is fully loaded with fuel, crew, cargo, passengers, etc.
Freight tonnage: 1 ton equals 40cu ft, a measure established in Elizabethan times.

Tun 60cu ft or 2,000lb, which measures only the capacity of the ship. In 'displacement tonnage' the tun equals 100cu ft.

Tuns burthen The number of tuns (originally of wine) a ship could carry. 'Tuns and tunnage' included the space between the casks.

Windward The direction from which the wind is blowing. See **Leeward**.

Yawl Type of fore-and-aft vessel with tall mainmast and a shorter aftermast. In a yawl the mizen is about a quarter the size of the mainsail, whereas in a ketch it is nearer half the size of the mainsail. The rudder post on a ketch is aft of the mizen mast, on a yawl it is forward of the mizen.

Unloading herring at Yarmouth in late 1937. Easy enough – but then just look at the strain on the face of the man in the middle.

SOURCES

INTRODUCTION

1. Charles Gibson: *The Story of the Ship* (Abelard Schuman, London, England, 1958).
2. C.R. Benstead: *Shallow Waters* (Robert Hale, London, England, 1958).

I MEN O' WAR

1. John Keegan: *The Price of Admiralty* (Hutchinson, London, England, 1988).
2. Paul Kennedy: *The Rise and Fall of British Naval Mastery* (Allen Lane, London, England, 1976).
3. Anthony Preston: *Dreadnought to Nuclear Submarine* (HMSO, London, England, 1980).
4. Randolph Pears: *British Battleships 1892–1957* (Putnam, London, England, 1957).
5. Sydney Poole: *Cruisers, A History of British Cruisers from 1889 to 1960* (Robert Hale, London, England, 1970).
6. Samuel Eliot Morison, quoted by Paul Kennedy.
7. Anthony Preston: *V & W Class Destroyers, 1917–1945* (Macdonald, London, England, 1971).
8. H.T. Lenton: *British Escort Ships* (Macdonald, London, England, 1974).

The feature on 'The Expendables' was based on interviews by Chris Durlacher for the programme, 'Classic Ships'.

II THE GREAT LINERS

1. Robert Gardiner and Ambrose Greenway (eds): *The Golden Age of Shipping, the Classic Merchant Ship 1900–1960* (Conway Maritime, London, England, 1994).
2. *Orient Line Guide*, quoted by Sarah Searight in *Steaming East* (The Bodley Head, London, England, 1991).
3. John M. Maber: *The Ship, Channel Packets and Ocean Liners* (HMSO, London, England, 1980).

See also:

Peter Smith: *Heritage of the Sea* (Balfour, St Ives, Huntingdon, England, 1974).

Fred Walker: *Song of the Clyde, A History of Clyde Shipbuilding* (Patrick Stephens, Cambridge, England, 1984).

III A LIFE ON THE OCEAN WAVE

1. Basil Greenhill in *The Ship: The Life and Death of the Merchant Sailing Ship* (HMSO, London, England, 1980).
2. Robert Gardiner and Ambrose Greenway (eds): *The Golden Age of Shipping, The Classic Merchant Ship 1900–1960* (Conway Maritime, London, England, 1994).
3. Tony Lane: *Grey Dawn Breaking, British Merchant Seamen in the Late 20th Century* (Manchester University Press, Manchester, England, 1986).
4. Tony Gloster: March 1995 issue of *Classic Boat* magazine.
5. Frank C. Brown: *London Ship Types* (East Ham Echo, London, England, 1938).
6. Euan Corlett: *The Ship: The Revolution in Merchant Shipping 1950–1980*, (HMSO, London, England, 1981).
7. Captain A.G. Course: *The Merchant Navy: A Social History* (Frederick Muller, London, England, 1963).
8. George Young: *Farewell to the Tramps* (Kommetjie, Cape Province, South Africa, 1982).
9. C.B.A. Behrens: *Merchant Shipping and the Demands of War* (HMSO, London, England, 1955).

See also:

Fred Walker: *Song of the Clyde, A History of Clyde Shipbuilding* (Patrick Stephens, Cambridge, England, 1984).

Robert Gardiner and Basil Greenhill: *The Merchant Steamship before 1900* (Conway Maritime, London, England, 1993).

IV BOATS AT WORK

1. C.R. Benstead, *Shallow Waters* (Robert Hale, London, England, 1958).
2. Eric McKee: *Working Boats of Britain* (Conway Maritime, London, England, 1983).
3. Michael Bouquet: *South-Eastern Sail* (David & Charles, Newton Abbot, England, 1972).
4. Frank C. Brown: *London Ship Types* (East Ham Echo, London, England, 1938).
5. Peter Smith: *Heritage of the Sea* (Balfour, St Ives, Huntingdon, England, 1974).
6. Pam Schweitzer (ed): *On the River: Memories of a Working River* (Age Exchange, London, England, 1989).
7. M.K. Stammers: *Tugs and Towage*. (Shire Publications, Princes Risborough, England, 1989).

See also:

M.J. Gaston: *Tugs and Towing* (P. Stephens, Yeovil, England, 1991).

Tony Gloster: 'The Twilight of the Trows', in the June 1995 issue of the *Boatman* magazine.

V THE FISHERMEN OF ENGLAND – AND SCOTLAND

1. Eric McKee: *Working Boats of Britain* (Conway Maritime, London, England, 1983).
2. C.R. Benstead: *Shallow Waters* (Robert Hale, London, England, 1958).
3. Keith Harris: *Hevva! Cornish Fishing in the Days of Sail* (Dyllansow Truran, Redruth, England, 1983).
4. Judy Brickhill talking to Jo O'Mahony for the programme, 'Classic Ships'.
5. Mike Smylie: April 1995 issue of the *Boatman*.
6. Jim Holmes: *A Drifterman's Diary* (privately published, Lowestoft, England, 1994).
7. John Rowe: *Cornwall in the Age of the Industrial Revolution* (Cornish Hillside Publications, St Austell, England, 1993).

8. Richard Carew, quoted by Dave Smart in *The Cornish Fishing Industry, A Brief History* (Tor Mark, Penrhyn, England, 1992).

9. Ibid.

10. Don Turtle talking to Jo O'Mahony for the programme, 'Classic Ships'.

11. David Butcher: *Following the Fishing* (David & Charles, Newton Abbot, England, 1987).

12. Dennis George interviewed by Jim Holmes.

13. Gloria Wilson: *Scottish Fishing Boats* (Hutton Press, Beverley, 1995).

See also:

K.W. Kent: *Herring Heydays* (SB Publications, Market Drayton, England, 1992).

John Leather on smacks and bawleys in the *Boatman*, June 1995 issue.

John Mellor and Robert Simper on Yarmouth shrimp boats in *Classic Boat*, March 1995 issue.

VI MESSING ABOUT IN BOATS

1. Pam Schweitzer:*On the River: Memories of a Working River* (Age Exchange, London, England, 1989).

2. A.P. Herbert: *A.P.H.: His Life and Times* (Heinemann, London, England, 1970).

3. Reginald Pound: *A.P. Herbert: A Biography* (Michael Joseph, London, England, 1970).

4. Reginald Bolland: *Victorians on the Thames* (Midas Books, Tunbridge Wells, England, 1974).

5. Peter Freebody interviewed by Peter Spectre in *Wooden Boat*, issue 57.

6. Interview with Martyn Nutland, the *Boatman* , April 1995 issue.

7. Angus Macdonald: 'The Golden Hind', *Classic Boat*, July 1995 issue.

8. June Dixon: *Uffa Fox, a Personal Biography* (Angus & Robertson, Brighton, England, 1978).

See also:

Nic Compton: 'Whistles over Windermere', *Classic Boat*, November 1994 issue.

VII SAIL, SEA, SNOBBERY – AND TRUE GRIT

1. E.K. Chatterton: *Sailing Ships* (Sidgwick & Jackson, London, England, 1909).

2. Donald M. Street: *The Ocean-Sailing Yacht* (David & Charles, Newton Abbot, England, 1974).

3. Anthony Heckstall-Smith: *Sacred Cowes* (Anthony Blond, London, England, 1965).

4. Junius Morgan, quoted by Ian Dear in *Enterprise to Endeavour: J-Class Yachts* (Editions INk, London, England, 1989).

5. Ian Dear on the Fastnet Race in *Classic Boat*, July 1995 issue.

See also:

Catalogue of photographs of Beken of Cowes.

GLOSSARY

1. C.R. Benstead, *Shallow Waters* (Robert Hale, London, England, 1958).

And so we say farewell . . . watching can be just as exhausting as rowing.

INDEX

Picture Acknowledgements

ALLSPORT (Mike Cooper) 15; ASSOCIATED PRESS 10–11; BEKEN OF COWES 23, 41, 47, 49, 53, 128–9, 130, 132–3; DAVID W. BEARE 90; D.J. MACKINNON 38, 79, 87, 113; EMPICS LTD 135; HULTON DEUTSCH 89, 92, 93, 95, 97, 100, 102, 110, 119, 136; KEEPER OF THE RECORDS OF SCOTLAND 61; KINEMA COLLECTION 73; KOS PICTURE SOURCE LTD 122, 134; SIR WILLIAM LITHGOW 62; MALCOLM FIFE 6, 63, 66, 70–1, 76; MANSELL COLLECTION, 45, 112; METHUEN CHILDREN'S BOOKS 106; NIKOS/CLASSIC BOAT 111, 114, 115, 118, 140; P&O CONTAINERS 67; POPPERFOTO 8, 21, 33, 42, 44, 52, 58, 80, 82–3, 84, 85, 98–9, 109 120, 121, 125, 126; RICHARD JOHNSTONE-BRYDEN 76; RICK TOMLINSON 14, 131; SCOTTISH FISHERIES MUSEUM TRUST LTD 103, 105; TELEGRAPH COLOUR LIBRARY Title page, 54–5, 57; TONY GLOSTER 117; TOPHAM PICTURE SOURCE Half title page, 12, 13, 16, 20, 24, 25, 26–7, 28, 29, 30–1, 32, 35, 46, 50, 51, 64, 74, 78, 108, 127; W. DOYLE 18